Integrating Technology

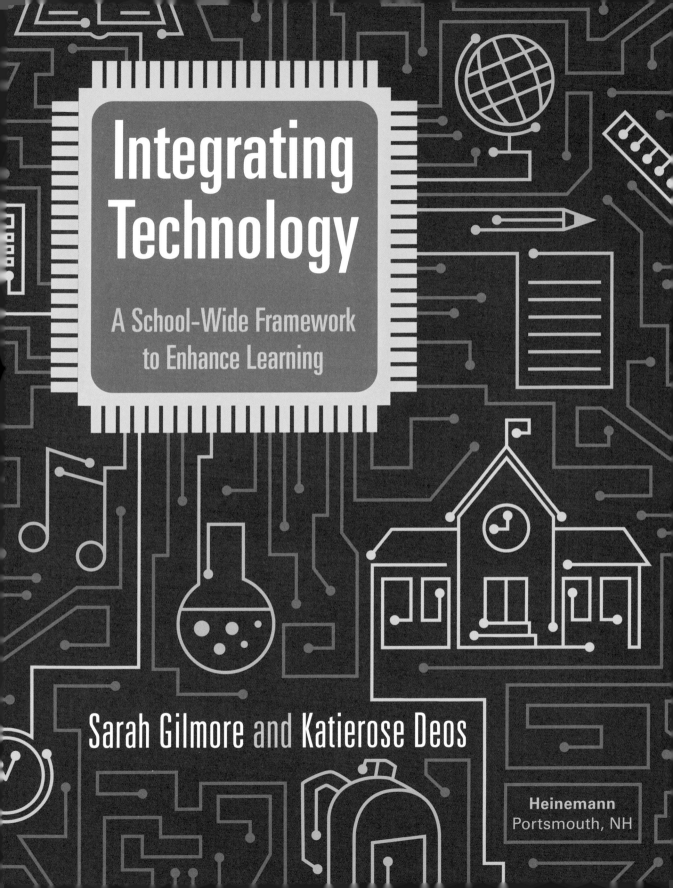

Integrating Technology

A School-Wide Framework to Enhance Learning

Sarah Gilmore and **Katierose Deos**

Heinemann
Portsmouth, NH

Heinemann

361 Hanover Street

Portsmouth, NH 03801–3912

www.heinemann.com

Offices and agents throughout the world

The authors and publisher wish to thank those who have generously given permission to reprint borrowed material:

ISTE Standards for Educators. Copyright © 2016 by ISTE (International Society for Technology in Education), iste.org. All rights reserved.

Cataloging-in-Publication Data is on file with the Library of Congress.

ISBN: 978-0-325-10952-7

Editor: Zoë Ryder White

Production Editor: Sonja S. Chapman

Cover and interior designs: Vita Lane

Typesetter: Shawn Girsberger

Manufacturing: Steve Bernier

Printed in the United States of America on acid-free paper

24   23   22   21   20   CGB   1   2   3   4   5

January 2020 printing

To Kerry, my husband and best friend,
thank you for believing in me enough
for the both of us.
—*Sarah*

To my parents, Peggy and Tony Deos, who
worked so hard to give me a positive start on
my journey.

And to my husband, Tom, for your continued
support along the way.
—*Katierose*

Contents

10 Taking Integration Forward

Online Resources

To access the online resources for *Integrating Technology,* either scan this QR code or visit Hein.pub/Tech-Resources.

Acknowledgments

This book could never have been written without the input, support, and guidance of many, many people. What's more, the *ideas* behind this book are the product of our experiences working alongside talented, insightful, and visionary educators from our own school and schools around the world.

We are beyond grateful to the leadership and administration at Berlin International School and Private Kant-Schulen (Germany), including Heather Sandin-Baumann, Michael Cunningham, Richard Eaton, and Andreas Wegener, for their support of us in both our teaching and leadership roles and the research and writing of this book. To Heather in particular, thank you for the belief and trust you have shown in us over these years: without your leadership and support this book would not exist! You, along with Dr. Helen Kelly, set the wheels in motion that have brought us to where we are today, by putting us both in our respective roles at Berlin International School. Who could have foreseen what would come of that decision?

To the teachers at Berlin International School, thank you for your openness to new ideas, for your willingness to experiment with technology and pedagogy, and for trusting us throughout this journey. You have made this experience one filled with growth both professionally and personally. It is because of each of you that we know more today about what good teaching is and where it can move to in the future. We are grateful also to Mike Yeung and Christian Siebert for informing our understanding of technology infrastructure and working patiently with us over the past several years.

To Lucy McMahan and Dawn Becker in particular, thank you for taking the time to read our drafts and give us such helpful feedback from a teacher perspective, and thank you also for always being ready and willing to try something new and push yourselves outside your comfort zones!

During the research phase of this book we interviewed educators, researchers, and experts from around the world and would like to thank the following people:

- Clara Alaniz and Suzana Spina of the Plano Independent School District, Texas

- Professor Field Rickards and Dr. Joanne Blannin of the University of Melbourne Graduate School of Education, Australia

- Professor Judy Robertson of the University of Edinburgh, Moray House School of Education, Scotland

- Professor Peter Williamson and Christine Bywater of Stanford Graduate School of Education, California

- Dr. James Robson of Oxford University Department of Education, England

For their roles in informing and guiding our wider thinking on technology, learning, and education in general, we are very grateful to Professor Guy Claxton, Cathryn Berger Kaye, and the International Baccalaureate Primary Years Programme, which has been a fundamental force in forming our view of and approach to learning and teaching over the past decade and more.

Our grateful thanks go to Rachel French, Diana van Mersbergen, Dr. Helen Kelly, Kate Birch, and Kerry Gilmore, for their time and effort in providing us with excellent feedback and careful proofreading of the manuscript. We are so grateful also to the incredible and talented people at Heinemann who have turned this book from an idea into a reality. This would not have been possible without the patient, thoughtful, and insightful editing of the wonderful Zoë Ryder White, Catrina Marshall's editorial coordination, production management from Sonja Chapman, design by Suzanne Heiser and Vita Lane, copyediting by Elizabeth Tripp, and marketing by Elizabeth Silvis.

Lastly and most importantly, we are so grateful to our families for the support, both practical and emotional, they have given us throughout the long and challenging process of writing this book.

From Sarah

Kerry Gilmore, your tireless editing and discussion of the content over the last two years have made this book so much better than it could have been without you, and I am sorry that listening to your entirely valid, carefully worded, helpful, constructive criticism turns me into a sulky teenager. You're the most patient person I know and I don't deserve you, but I will keep on trying to. Thank you.

Thank you to my beautiful and amazing babies, Mara and Freya. Mara, thank you for long naps so I could write, and Freya, thank you for a very solid deadline to finish writing! I hope one day you'll both read it and be proud of your mama.

From Katierose

Thank you to my husband for your endless patience, support, and encouragement. You continue to be the stable balance within my life, and I can honestly say that with you, I am the best version of myself. You are loved, always.

To my three children, Eila, Owen, and Maeve, thank you for continuing to remind me whom this book is really for and why we, as education professionals, have a duty to continue thinking, developing, and evolving our practice.

Everyone that passes through my life changes a piece of me, but the core of who I am has been built from the love and unending support of my parents, Margaret and Anthony Deos. No words could possibly capture all that you have been and continue to be to me. So, thank you for working with me through all the small moments, for weathering the storm of life's big moments, and for building a fortress of four fantastic siblings for me to go through life with. Tony, Holly, Julia, and Jackie, you are irreplaceable, and I feel so lucky to have you by my side.

Introduction

*A very little key will open
a very heavy door.*

Charles Dickens,
Hunted Down

No matter where, what, or whom we teach, the challenges we face as teachers in our classrooms often leave us feeling that we have far too much to do and far too little time. The curriculum feels increasingly crowded; the demands of standardized testing and academic rigor—as well as pressure to emphasize attainment in "core" subjects such as math and literacy—push out elements of education that teachers know to be extremely important, such as the arts, play, and personal and social education. We teach classes of twenty- or even thirty-plus students, some of whom may have complex needs and *all* of whom have unique strengths with individual requirements and challenges. Despite this, our aim is to differentiate learning and try our best to ensure that no child in our care will fail to meet their potential.

This is a daunting, enormously important task, and it isn't getting any easier. In an increasingly global world, our student body grows more diverse, the social demands on children outside of school continuously increase, and the expectations of what the future citizens of the world will be able to do grow ever more complex. Many teachers, when faced with technology as another element to consider, understandably wonder how, if we can't find time for play or music, we can find time for technology.

In many schools, technology is still seen and treated as an add-on, and the reasons for this are clear: technology *was* an add-on—until recently—in life and therefore in education. It was to a much greater extent a luxury or supplement to a generally offline life, but the role of technology in our lives beyond school has changed drastically from when IT (information technology) or computing skills or keyboard skills were introduced to the curriculum. Today we use technology to shop, to stay in contact with our loved ones, to express our opinions, to make friends, and even to fall in love. We make beautiful music and art with technology. We use it to design and create tools to make the world a safer, healthier, and better place. We (and our students, for better or for worse) can, and do, learn about any topic that interests us *instantly* through Wikipedia, YouTube, or Google, and technology runs every major system in the world from health to finance. In fact, technology has become a seamlessly embedded and integrated element of nearly every facet of our lives *except* for teaching and learning.

The wonderful thing about effective technology integration is that when we plan and implement it thoughtfully and purposefully, it is the opposite of an add-on. It truly makes teaching and classroom learning more meaningful, relevant, and effective for students and for teachers. Technology integration is an incredibly powerful tool that provides choice and individualization, supports the day-to-day and exceptional needs of students, and increases the efficiency of communication and assessment. With it, we can enhance and revolutionize traditional teaching ideas and approaches to enable students to engage more deeply with the concepts and skills they need to be successful learners.

Yet we are at a challenging point in the journey of technology and its role in education. It is inarguable that technology is becoming more and more important in the world beyond school, but significant barriers exist for teachers and students in achieving the educational potential it offers. A coherent pedagogical vision for technology's role in learning has, until now, been absent from teacher education and professional development. Financial inequity in school funding continues to have far-reaching consequences for classroom practice and student outcomes, such that even while more and more money is being spent on technology in schools globally, access to technology remains a luxury for many schools and families. We recognize that at a time when many teachers have insufficient basic resources like paper, books, and even furniture, we cannot underestimate the role that access and privilege play in the discussion about technology use and integration, yet we also know that in time the question is not *whether* technology will become more widely and deeply embedded in your educational context, or even *to what extent*, but only whether that technology will be used in a way that genuinely benefits your students.

There is a lot of work to be done at the higher levels of government and further education to begin to develop a fairer, more sustainable, and forward-thinking approach to how technology is resourced, taught, and implemented both nationally and internationally. It is time for the barriers that teachers and students face with regard to access and use of technology, which is increasingly expected of graduates and employees in every field, to begin to fall.

With so many factors out of our control, it might seem that integration is an unnecessary or unrealistic goal, especially if you are working in a context where access to technology is limited or the culture isn't supportive of technology. But we do have the power to overcome some of these barriers: our experience—and our message—is that whatever technology you have in your school or classroom, it *can* be integrated in a way that enhances learning for your students. Effective technology integration is not so much about what resources you have (although of course it's great to have a whole-class set of tablets or a school makerspace or a fleet of robots) as it is about being committed to planning for and using the resources you *do* have to give your students learning experiences that meet their needs in the classroom and prepare them for life beyond it. Even if you have just a single PC, or your school's Internet service is unreliable or nonexistent, with a deeper understanding of the purpose of technology integration, with the knowledge of how to plan for, scaffold, and use it, and with the desire to harness the power of the technology you have for the benefit of student learning, you can take what is happening in your classroom and make it even better for your students *and* yourself.

This is a book for everyone involved in education, because the conversation of why and how we can use technology to enhance learning is not just a pedagogical conversation, or a leadership conversation, or a financial conversation: it is an educational conversation. At every level, from superintendent, to teacher, to school leader, to policy maker, we need to have a shared understanding of the foundation of the issues and possibilities at the heart of technology integration. Teachers need to be thinking about what their leaders and their state are doing to support and implement technology integration in order to ask questions and advocate for support. Leaders and administrators need to know what the purposes and possibilities are for daily effective integration of technology in order to put structures in place to support it. We all need to be asking questions and engaging in a shared dialogue about what technology integration is, what we believe about it, and what its purpose is so we can make systematic, meaningful, sustainable, and manageable change.

Throughout, you will find that we repeatedly refer to the importance of context with regard to how you might choose, or be permitted, to implement the ideas we present. This is because educational norms, pressures, requirements, and opportunities differ so greatly around the world. In some countries or educational systems teachers must—or must not— use certain apps and tools. In some countries, pedagogical approach, written curriculum, or organizational structure is highly prescribed, while in others it is not. As such, much as we might wish to, we cannot provide the ideal technology integration curriculum, the ideal resourcing structure, or even the ideal technology vision and approach: only you can take the bigger picture we share and apply it to your own unique context.

Our belief is that wherever you are in the world, and whatever your role, be that a teacher, a professor, a leader, or an administrator at the school, district, state, or even national level, you will benefit from this book. We encourage you to read every chapter, whether or not it directly relates to your role. At the end of each chapter you will find questions and reflection prompts targeted to different educational aims and roles, to support you in seeing how the content of the chapter relates to you professionally. You will also find references throughout the book to online resources in the form of regularly updated lists of digital approaches and tools to supplement and support the ideas and information in the book, as well as a reflection and discussion guide. Additionally, you can connect with educators, ask questions, share stories, and more on Twitter using the hashtag #Intechgrate or join the Facebook group for readers at https://www.facebook.com/groups/IntechgrateBookCommunity. Educational change requires all of us involved in education to participate and collaborate. We invite and encourage you to reflect, share, question, and be a part of the discussion.

Charles Dickens wrote, "A very little key will open a very heavy door" (2017/1859, 11). We believe that technology, when it is used effectively with purpose and vision, can be the little key that opens the very heavy door to enhancing student learning.

01

Purposeful Technology Integration

It's Not What You Have, It's How You Use It

This book is a response to the unanswered question that has increasingly confronted teachers and leaders: What is the role of technology in education? What can it do, and what can't it do? How can we use what we have most effectively to benefit students?

We have come to believe that technology has the potential to be an immensely powerful tool for learning. We can use it to

- facilitate and expand pathways for student collaboration, reflecting the way that we work together in the world beyond school;

- provide context and connection to support students in constructing an understanding of big concepts and ideas;

- help students build resilience, agency, and curiosity through problem-solving, design, and exploration by building, iterating, and taking action around big issues; and

- provide manageable, meaningful options for communicating and sharing learning that meet the needs of our students and encourage creativity and critical thinking.

Meeting that potential means that our use of technology in education needs to evolve. While a great deal of inequity remains in terms of funding for and access to technology, spending on technology in schools has increased enormously in recent years. With technology becoming cheaper and more ubiquitous, its prominence in the classroom will continue to increase. Technology is quickly becoming embedded in every subject at any age, yet there is a lack of educational discourse about its purpose and how best to use it to meet that purpose. For many years the focus has been resolutely on the *what* of technology: the number of devices, the best apps, top-fifty lists of tools, and professional development that emphasizes tools over teaching. However, simply having technology in classrooms is not enough to realize its potential. If we are going to use technology in meaningful and effective ways, then all of us, as teachers of and with technology, need to be supported in shifting our focus from the *what* of the tools to the *how* and, critically, the *why*.

If you, as a second-grade, eighth-grade, science, music, or any other kind of teacher, are asking yourself, "What does that have to do with me?" the answer is that *you too* are a teacher of technology!

For teachers who feel uncomfortable using technology, or uneasy with the role of technology in the classroom, the idea that we are technology teachers as well as homeroom teachers or specialist teachers might not be a welcome one. But, with technology becoming a feature of most classrooms to an ever-increasing degree, we all share a responsibility—and an opportunity—to make sure that it is being used effectively, safely, and responsibly for the benefit of our students.

We stand now at a turning point in education where we can expand our focus from putting technology in the classroom to thinking critically about how we are using that technology to enhance student learning.

What Technology Integration Is and Why It Matters

In recent years a shift away from the concept of teaching technology to that of integrating technology has begun. In essence, what this distinction boils down to is a move away from treating technology primarily as a skills-based, disciplinary subject that students *do* (e.g., "We have IT next period") to seeing it as something that they *use to enhance* how they learn something else. With an integrated approach to technology education we treat technology as a tool that we can apply in all subjects and to various tasks, for the purpose of enhancing the learning process.

This does not mean that technology is not still also a subject in its own right: there will always be technology-specific skills and understandings our students need to have to be able to use it effectively, particularly as they move through school.

> We define *technology integration* as follows: the intentional planning and purposeful use of technology within education to enhance the content, process, or product related to the teaching and learning.

What it means is that as the nature and application of technology beyond school have evolved, so too must our approach to how we use and teach with it. Technology skills, such as coding—or even how to use a mouse or type accurately—still matter, but there needs to be a balance in how we teach and model these skills to make them as meaningful to students as possible. This will help students learn to make informed, discerning choices about when, why, and how to use technology in and beyond the classroom.

This is why an integrated approach to technology is so valuable for learning: it puts student learning at the center as its purpose. It moves us away from a device-centric approach of technology for technology's sake to technology for *learning's* sake. Technology integration doesn't mean using technology all the time or, necessarily, more than you already do; it means using it purposefully, in ways and at times that make sense. When technology is integrated effectively it supports student learning in all its forms, allowing teachers to break down learning barriers and enhance wider teaching and learning.

What Is *Effective* Technology Integration?

Efficacy can be a tricky and subjective concept in education, since whether you consider something to have been effective or not really depends on what you hoped to achieve by doing it. We believe that the measure of truly effective technology integration is whether it enhances student learning, and this in turn relies upon a different conceptualization of what technology's purpose and role in learning can and should be. In the past, educational focus on technology in the classroom has been on computer-based tests, digital worksheets, technology skills, "research" (generally in the form of googling), and defining technology's value by its ability to boost test scores. Instead, we need to explore technology's ability to support students in the *process* of learning and to help them develop the disposition to be successful learners.

When we think about technology's purpose in the classroom, and how we can leverage its strengths to help students develop the ability to learn successfully, we frame it around what we call the *3 Cs of learning*: communicating, collaborating, and constructing understanding. (See Figure 1.1.)

The 3 Cs of Student Learning:
Communicating, Collaborating, and Constructing Understanding

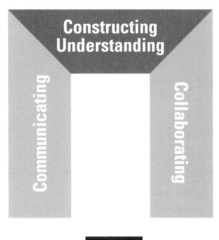

Figure 1.1

Communication is vital to classroom learning, and we think about it in two ways: our communication as teachers and the communication we ask of our students. We ask students to communicate constantly: with themselves, each other, us, and the wider world. In Chapter 4 we take a deep look at the technology approaches and teaching tools that can enhance and facilitate how students communicate, including reflecting and self-assessing, demonstrating learning, participating in daily classroom activities and discussions, and digital citizenship.

Collaboration is the ability to work with others to create, solve problems, and learn. Whether within students' own class or school, or with other students, experts, and adults outside the school, working collaboratively is an extremely valuable skill for learning and one that is highly valued in adult life and work. In Chapter 5 we explore how you can encourage, facilitate, and support responsible, meaningful, and innovative collaboration through technology integration.

Communication and collaboration are twin pillars supporting the ultimate goal of learning: constructing understanding. Being able to transfer learning and construct deep understanding relies on students having the opportunity and support to attach content to concepts and make connections between classroom learning and real life. This is what allows our students take the facts, knowledge, and skills they have learned out of theory and into reality; it changes their learning from abstract to concrete. We can use technology in ways that allow our students to communicate and collaborate more effectively and more seamlessly. This helps us break down barriers and create the best conditions we can so they can make connections between ideas, share thoughts and questions, learn from peers and adults around the world, and take learning beyond the classroom, into the world.

How Can We Integrate Technology Effectively?

Effective technology integration isn't about what you have; it's about how you use it. And how you use it depends on so much more than just curriculum, or just devices, or just pedagogy. It depends on having a purpose-based, holistic, and student-centered approach to integrating all aspects of technology in learning.

The process of developing that vision for technology integration and realizing it in a sustainable way can be long and challenging, but we believe it is worthwhile. As educators and as writers, our aim in our practice and in this book is to share what we have learned in our teaching and our work with others about how and why technology integration can make a positive impact on learning and to present an effective framework for schools and teachers.

We emphasize the need for a holistic approach to technology integration at the school level, but we also believe that there is a need for a holistic approach at all levels in education. We hope that this book will further illustrate the need to evaluate how we plan for and implement technology integration from the policy level, through research, funding, and teacher training programs so that we can start to build a shared vision for the role of technology in student learning and work as a system to make that vision a reality.

The Intechgrate Model

Often, technology integration is discussed or considered at the classroom level, as in common questions such as "What are teachers and students doing with technology?" and "What do we want them to do in the classroom?" Of course, if we want to be successful in using technology to enhance and facilitate the 3 Cs of learning, then planning for and scaffolding effective technology integration in classroom teaching is critical, and we explore different aspects of this in detail within several chapters of this book. However, we believe that for technology to truly enhance teaching and learning, it has to be integrated not just at the pedagogical (classroom) level but at an educational (system) level in a way that is intentional, sustainable, and, most important, meaningful.

Effective technology integration is not dependent on either tools *or* pedagogy *or* teacher mindset *or* curriculum *or* leadership. It is dependent on all those things and more, to differing degrees, all at the same time. The factors that affect how or whether technology is used effectively in classrooms are not independent of each other: they are fundamentally, inextricably connected and interdependent. When there is a disconnect or imbalance in these factors, technology cannot meet its potential to enhance student learning.

You might, for example, see this imbalance in schools where there is a mismatch between the visions for technology and teaching—specifically what the technology, or more general curriculum, demands from teachers and what teachers are actually able to do with the resources and infrastructure available to them.

We developed the Intechgrate Model to support educators and the education system to avoid these disconnects by sharing a holistic, transferable vision and framework for technology integration that embraces and utilizes the interconnected nature of the following six components:

- *Purpose*: With purpose you define for yourself and your context the ideal current and future role of technology in the classroom and in education more widely. How should it support and benefit students and the learning process?

- *Mindset*: Our mindset encapsulates the many factors that form our conscious and unconscious beliefs about technology and how these beliefs influence our practice in the classroom.

- *Pedagogy*: *Pedagogy* refers to the strategies, approaches, and processes we as teachers actively and deliberately employ to plan for, scaffold, and realize effective technology integration in the classroom.

- *Curriculum*: Our curriculum includes the written standards (at the school level, national level, or international level) that underlie teaching and assessment and the ways in which we can choose to approach them in the classroom to support technology integration.

- *Resources and infrastructure*: Taking a pedagogical approach to resources and infrastructure means developing and maintaining physical technology tools to deliberately support technology integration practice within and beyond the classroom.

- *Leadership*: Effective technology integration leadership refers to the development and provision of support and direction for technology integration through each of the other elements of the Intechgrate Model, at all levels of educational leadership.

The Intechgrate Model: A Holistic Approach to Developing and Supporting Technology Integration in Education

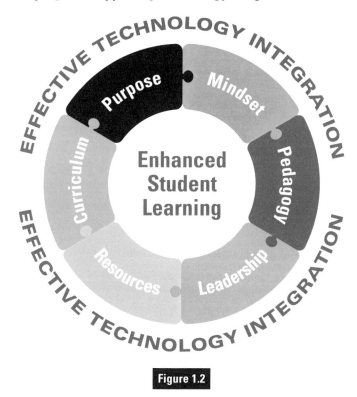

Figure 1.2

The model is structured like a jigsaw puzzle because that is essentially what effective technology integration is: without all of the pieces, the picture at the center of it all, which is enhanced student learning, is lost (see Figure 1.2).

In the coming chapters we will focus on each of these elements in detail, presenting you with our vision for why they matter, how they connect, how they influence the effectiveness of technology integration, and how you can take steps to develop effective technology integration within your practice or your school. You will find that this book is not a how-to handbook or a prescription for how you should integrate technology in your specific context. Instead, we hope it will function as a prompt for critical thinking and discussion and as a guide for educators and education as a whole to begin to rethink technology's role in learning and how we can work systemically and holistically to realize that role. Like technology itself, this book is a tool that can be used to enhance and support student learning.

Reflection

To access the online resources including the Reflection and Forward Thinking Guide for Integrating Technology, *either scan the QR code on page ix or visit Hein.pub/ Tech-Resources.*

At the end of each chapter you will find a reflection section like this one, with questions designed to prompt thinking or discussion. We also include an online resource to support further reflection and forward thinking. We recommend that you take your time to think and make notes for yourself, but we also encourage you to participate in a wider conversation with other readers by visiting our Facebook group at https://www.facebook.com /groups/IntechgrateBookCommunity and following us on Twitter at hashtag #Intechgrate.

- *If your goal is supporting student learning:* In your past experience, when has technology been most and least effective in supporting or enhancing student learning?

- *If your goal is supporting professional learning:* What opportunities currently exist within your school's professional development sessions or structures to begin or continue the discussion of technology integration?

- *If your goal is supporting curriculum development:* Is the purpose of technology integration specifically, and learning more generally, a core element of the curricula in your context? If not, why not? How would it be different if it were?

- *If your goal is supporting organizational systems and structures:* What impact, positive or negative, does the way your technology systems, resources, and infrastructure are organized have on purposeful and effective technology integration?

02

The Research on Technology in Education

T wo of the biggest concerns we hear from parents and educators when it comes to the role of technology in schools are the perceived dangers of screen time and whether technology is beneficial, neutral, or harmful to student outcomes. For many, these fears are typically informed or fueled by news articles and opinion pieces that draw on examples of research that support whichever narrative will drive the highest readership—and that rarely represent the research in all its complexity. Research into human beings—whether about education, cognitive development, or anything else—is by nature complex and nuanced, because humans are complex and nuanced, and so are influences from the world around us.

In any research, some questions have been asked and answered, some questions have been asked but could not be answered, and some questions have *not even yet been asked*. This presents a tricky task for us educators, attempting to pick apart what the research says, what it doesn't say, and what all that means, let alone whether the research is high-quality and unbiased.

In this chapter we address these two main areas of concern and try to sum up some of what the research says, what it doesn't say, and what its implications are for technology integration.

Screen Time

Screen time, as a phrase, is almost exclusively used in a negative context, primarily in news reports raising alarm over the dangers and risks posed to children's physical and social well-being from time spent on digital devices. In recent years a belief has developed that either all screen time is inherently bad for children, or there is a set amount of screen time that is safe for children, above which they will suffer harm. The problems with these beliefs are that they suggest that all children of all ages have the same needs and vulnerabilities (they do not) and that all screen time is the same (it is not). As a society we use the term *screen time* to encompass so much, yet it means so little: screen time can mean watching TV or writing a book. Even "watching TV" can mean watching a violent movie or something with flashing lights, loud music, and a frenetic pace, or it can mean watching *Sesame Street*, *Mister Rogers' Neighborhood*, or *Blue Planet*. Trying to draw conclusions about all screen time for all children is impossible, because there are too many variables in both the screens and the children.

So, how do we make sense of the research and stories we are reading, and how do we make responsible decisions about screen time in our homes and classrooms for the benefit of our children?

There are three factors we need to consider when we read and think about screen time: the age of the child, what is happening on the screen, and what is *not* happening while the child is using the screen.

The American Academy of Pediatrics (AAP) released a policy statement in 2016 titled "Media and Young Minds," which summarized the research into the effects of time spent using digital media on infants through five-year-old children and laid out recommendations for the quantity and type of screen time for children in this age bracket. The AAP advised parents that children under two should ideally have no screen time (apart from video chatting with relatives with parental guidance) and that children between two and five years of age should limit screen time to one hour per day. It also advised that when children are allowed screen time, it should be with high-quality educational apps or TV programs that are not too fast paced, and it should end at least an hour before bedtime. This is because the brains of babies and young children are in a critical phase of development where poor-quality or excessive use of screens can do real damage. As children age, and their cognitive development changes, the risks and potential rewards of screen time change, and the guidelines for safe time limits increase.

However, it is important that we recognize that we simply cannot reduce all time spent looking at a screen down to a single concept of screen time. Reading an e-book is self-evidently different in terms of potential gains and risks than playing a game, and even the risks and rewards of game playing depend greatly on the quality and purpose of the game. Can we really say that reading a book on a screen is less valuable than reading a book on paper, simply because of the medium? Is the time spent playing a collaborative problem-solving game on a screen more or less antisocial than the time spent reading a book alone? And when we see headlines that suggest screen time causes terrifying problems for our children and students, such as cancer, obesity, diabetes, or language delays, what are we to make of those headlines?

Well, the key behind understanding the headlines and what they mean for educational technology use is threefold: (1) if possible, read the research the news article is based on, (2) bear in mind that correlation does not equal causation (more on this shortly), and (3) remember that headlines need to be significantly more interesting and dramatic than the research they are based on tends to be!

Take, for example, this very alarming tabloid headline: "Switch Off: Kids Who Spend Too Much Time Staring at Screens 'at Greater Risk of 12 Deadly Cancers'" (McDermott 2018). While the headline infers that technology is the cause of the issue, the World Cancer Research Fund (2018) report on which the article is based makes it clear that the technology itself is not causing cancer. Rather, it says, obesity and weight gain are the true danger factors in determining increased cancer risks, and it draws a correlation between screen time, exposure to junk food advertising, and sedentary lifestyles as risk factors for these issues. This might seem a subtle distinction, but it is a crucial one. If we fail to understand the true cause of the issue (junk food, advertising, and insufficient exercise), simply "switching off," as the headline commands, won't necessarily help. We need to know what the true issues are so we can take proactive steps to address or avoid them when helping kids manage their social time and meals.

We see this oversimplification repeated time and time again in headlines about screen time, and it comes down to one simple fact: correlation does not equal causation. While screen time might be a *risk factor* for what it indicates about a child's wider behaviors, it has never been shown to be the cause of the kinds of negative impacts that parents and teachers are rightly so concerned about.

What we think is finally being made very clear in some research (Orben and Przybylski 2019)—but much less clear in the news as yet—is this: screens themselves, and even what is on them, generally, are not the true cause of harm. Simply looking at screens is not harmful to school-aged children; screens are just things.

What is harmful is *missing out on the activities they aren't doing because they are using screens* and the influences they are exposed to *through* the screen, such as junk food advertising.

The AAP's report makes it clear that young children who spend hours watching TV or playing games on iPads are missing out on face-to-face, hands-on play and communication time that is crucial to their development. For older children and teenagers this is just as applicable in different ways. When screen time takes the place of regular dinner-time family conversation, that is harmful to children. When screen time takes the place of regular exercise, fresh air, or social interaction, that is harmful to children. When screen time takes the place of high-quality teaching—opportunities to think critically, be creative, solve problems, and collaborate in the classroom—that is harmful to children.

This means that we need to take a balanced and deliberate approach to technology's use in the classroom. Screens should never take the place of high-quality teaching; they should enrich it, based on student need. Digital worksheets, online drills, chatting, and surfing the Internet are rarely valuable uses of students' time, and simply going one-to-one (one device per student) without a vision for technology's role in education is an approach that runs the risk of being more about screen time than learning time. When technology is integrated in a purpose-based, deliberate way, the mind-set, curriculum, pedagogy, resourcing, and leadership work together so that technology is never replacing teaching or high-quality learning time; it is enhancing it.

Student Outcomes

All of us within the education field are driven by the goal to help our students to learn, to grow, to question, and to be successful in and beyond school. It is a vital aspect of our professional diligence that we should question whether or not new tools and approaches are going to help our students achieve that success. Following that, we immediately ask, "How do we define and measure success?" and when it comes to learning and schooling, this is no simple matter.

Many schools and teachers are under constant pressure to demonstrate that students are learning, but the evidence gathered about learning is almost always over a short-term cycle: comparing measurable outcomes from the start of the year with measurable outcomes from the end of the year or, at most, over the course of their time in school. When those measurable outcomes show a positive increase, this indicates to the public and the government that the school and the teacher have educational value. As a result, the educational focus shifts from long-term learning outcomes to short-term testing outcomes. Learning is a marathon, but testing is a sprint: what we really need to be questioning is how what we do in the classroom affects our students' learning, in the bigger sense, over a long period of time. *How* they learn, not necessarily *what* they learn, will determine how successful they are through their entire educational journey and their lives beyond.

Increasingly, the how of learning is becoming a more common topic of research, for example, through Project Zero of the Harvard Graduate School of Education. Since it was founded in 1967 by Nelson Goodman, well-known scientists from multiple disciplines have been working together to explore how humans think, express themselves, develop, and, of course, learn.

This work has led to groundbreaking concepts, such as Gardner's multiple intelligences framework (2011) and Perkins' and Ritchhart's work on visible thinking (Perkins 2003; Ritchhart, Church, and Morrison 2011) and cultures of thinking (Ritchhart 2015), that are leading us to think differently about the true nature of intelligence and learning. One of the key concepts behind the research is the idea that intelligence, and being successful as a learner, is less concrete and unchanging than we used to believe. If we believe that how successful you will be depends primarily on your IQ, which supposedly doesn't change a great deal after age eight (Tough 2014), or your academic abilities, then it makes sense to emphasize abilities-based teaching approaches and testing. However, research is beginning to show that while focusing on these aspects may be a good way of teaching our students to be good at school, they are not necessarily the best approaches for teaching our students to learn in the long term and to be able to actually use that learning beyond school. Instead, researchers like Arthur Costa and Bena Kallick (2008), Guy Claxton (2017), and those at Harvard's Project Zero take what is called a dispositional view of learning. Learning dispositions are the common traits and characteristics that students draw upon to be successful learners in a sense that is broader and longer term than can be measured in end-of-term tests: resilience, open-mindedness, creativity, curiosity, and so on. Students who have the support and opportunity to foster these skills throughout their educational journey *learn how to learn*, for the long term, into college or careers and beyond.

Measuring Technology's Impact on Outcomes

In 2015 the Organisation for Economic Co-operation and Development (OECD) released a report called *Students, Computers and Learning: Making the Connection*. This report became the basis for a huge number of headlines and articles that communicated variations on the alarming statement that technology had been proven to have little to no positive effect on student learning or might even be harmful to student learning. Many educators and members of the public have since been exposed to that message but not necessarily the specifics of the research behind it. It explored access to, and familiarity with, technology in the home and in school, the impact of socioeconomic status on technology access, student skill level in reading and math, and what the researchers called the "Index of ICT use at school," which cataloged the data about the time students spent engaged in nine specific IT activities.

As we saw with the screen-time issue, headlines often make big, bold, sweeping statements, but research is rarely bold and sweeping: researchers naturally tend to ask questions that can actually be answered, and questions about learning in general, as we've said, are extremely complex and nuanced. When we see alarming, definitive, or sweeping headlines about research on any topic it is important we look at what questions the research was truly asking and, crucially, which were not asked. What kinds of data were being collected and over what time frame? How big was the study?

The range of factors that influence student outcomes is truly enormous: leadership style, teacher attitudes and approaches, socioeconomic status, school culture, educational policy, and everything else that can influence how a human thinks, behaves, and learns. This is why research questions are by definition narrow and why they tend to favor collecting data that is as quantifiable as possible.

In this particular OECD study, the research focused specifically on analyzing the relationship between the quantity of "ICT" devices in schools (e.g., laptops, tablets, and desktops), the time spent using those devices, and students' standardized test scores in reading and math. The key finding that caused such alarm was that it appeared that students in schools with more technology, and who spent more time using that technology, fared worse on these tests on average.

But does that mean that technology is, as the headlines suggested, harmful to learning?

Firstly, we can infer a great deal about the OECD's understanding of technology from the activities the report included in its "Index of ICT Use." Students were asked how long they spent browsing the Internet, emailing, chatting online, downloading, uploading, or posting to the school's website versus how much time they spent "drilling" (intensively practicing skills) online during class time. Just as it isn't screens themselves that are harmful to children's development but what that screen time is replacing, it isn't technology that is harmful to learning—it is what is being done with that technology *instead of high-quality learning*.

The activities chosen for the OECD "Index of ICT Use" are all task-based, and they lack any connection to purpose or more meaningful learning objectives. They offer no opportunity for students to problem solve, think critically, collaborate, or be creative. To us it is not surprising that students who spent more time engaged in low-quality learning tasks, whether on- or offline, suffered on tests. If we replace activities like "online drilling" with "worksheets," "uploading files" with "putting work in binders," and "chatting online" with "chatting offline," it seems obvious that students who spend more time engaged in activities like these, regardless of the platform, will have poorer outcomes than students who spend that time engaging in high-quality, challenging learning activities.

Secondly, the report is interested only in technology's impact on what can be measured through attainment-focused standardized assessment. Test scores are a natural and logical choice for large-scale research into student outcomes because they are quantifiable, easy to compare, and easy to gather over large sample sizes. However, standardized reading and math scores can tell us only so much about a student's learning. They rarely tell us how well a student understands the topic or the student's background knowledge, and they don't tell us about a student's learning behaviors or disposition or about the child's ability to think critically or apply solutions to complex problems. They don't tell us how creative a student is, how well the student collaborates, or how they communicate. And when we ask only how technology impacts test scores when it is used in limited ways, that is all we find out.

The true finding of the OECD's report is very simple: quantity does not equal quality. Simply having more devices, spending more time using those devices, and substituting low-quality offline teaching practices with low-quality online teaching practices does not translate into improved meaningful student outcomes. We wholeheartedly agree with that finding! But that does not mean that technology is harmful to learning: it means that technology, when it is provided without a plan for use, when it is used without student learning at the core of its purpose, may be harmful to student learning.

Unfortunately, academic research has yet to begin to really explore the question of how the technology we already have could be used *differently* to enhance or support the learning process. Partly, this is because the learning process itself is so complex and not fully understood. Partly it might be because it would be so challenging to isolate the impact of integrated technology, specifically, in a classroom setting from the impacts of so many other elements simultaneously affecting outcomes, such as teacher practices, leadership, student backgrounds, and pedagogical approach. Partly it is because research relies on *measuring and quantifying*, and we don't yet know how to measure and quantify the learning process itself (rather than its outcomes), let alone technology's potential impact on it.

The Takeaways for Educators

These are questions that research will continue to grapple with, we hope, because technology investment in education continues to grow year after year. While official figures on this front are difficult to come by, and vary quite widely in the press, we can see by simple observation that more and more classrooms and schools have increased access to devices over the past three to five years, with one-to-one ratios of devices to students becoming ever more the norm. However, if we do not address *how* those devices are used, we are not likely to see improved student outcomes. As we've said, effective classroom technology integration isn't about what you have; it's about how you use it. We don't need to rush to invent or buy new technology to enhance student learning: we need to learn to use the technology we already have in a more meaningful, purposeful, and effective way.

For this to happen, the discussion about education needs to be more farsighted and more inclusive than it currently is, and it needs to be focused on what education is supposed to be about: learning. We need to take a long, hard look at what we mean when we talk about student outcomes. We have to ask ourselves what success really is, whether what we are typically measuring in education today is about schooling or about learning, and whether it has long-term meaning for our students.

Whether or not technology is a valuable tool for student outcomes depends on us, as educators and leaders. We face many challenges in education, and we all want our students to be successful, but the research has shown us that just putting more computers into schools won't achieve that goal. However, we believe that finding the bigger vision for the role of technology in education and addressing how we train and support new and existing teachers to realize that vision in the classroom, might.

Reflection

- Concerning screen time and student outcomes specifically, what opinions did you already have about these topics? How have those opinions and concerns affected your teaching practice or your personal actions with technology?

- When reading about educational research in general, how does the educational reading you engage with affect your mind-set related to education or, more specifically, technology within education?

Mindset

Teachers, Teaching, and Technology

Our beliefs affect our actions in profound ways, in every area of our lives. Human life is intricately layered and textured. Our experiences from birth through adolescence and adulthood fundamentally define our beliefs—and shape our approaches and actions.

We accept this in our day-to-day lives, yet it is rare for us in our role as teachers to have the opportunity to reflect on the impact our experiences, beliefs, and mindset have on our approaches and actions in the classroom. Teachers are dedicated, caring professionals and we strive to be consistent and objective when applying the curriculum developments, strategies, and ideologies we have been trained in, but can we ever really teach in a way that removes all influence from our personal beliefs? And would we really want to?

We believe that we can't (and shouldn't) completely compartmentalize who we are and what we believe as individuals from what happens in our classrooms. The unique and personal approaches that teachers bring to their students make learning personal and meaningful, create human connections, establish educational communities, and make learning truly enriching.

However, it *is* important to be aware of what those influences are and how they affect how we teach. With that awareness, we can take a critical look at the impact those influences inevitably have on our teaching and where it might be time to address how our beliefs and experiences could be restricting the development of our practice. Therefore, in this chapter we will

- look at how our beliefs, experiences, and approaches relate to technology;

- evaluate our technology mindset and its influence on our teaching practice;

- consider some of the factors that create and sustain mindsets; and

- suggest some approaches for developing personal and institutional mindsets around teaching with and through technology.

The Role of Mindset in Teacher Use of Technology

It is a certainty that before now you will have come into contact with a number of differing viewpoints on technology and, more specifically, technology within the classroom. There is a wide spectrum of beliefs and experiences among teachers when it comes to technology, and you may see this at work in your own school, with some teachers using technology frequently to support instruction, some not at all, and many falling somewhere in between. Research (Drent and Meelissen 2008, Prestridge 2012, Sang et al. 2010) clearly shows that a teacher's personal beliefs about technology are pivotal in how willing the teacher is to use technology in the classroom and, crucially, how *effectively* they do so.

This variety in teacher beliefs can be a powerful tool to support school development and professional learning if addressed through collaborative, professional conversations as well as training and, eventually, policy. As teachers we have a responsibility to be critical of new initiatives and ideas and take a considered approach when we implement them in our classrooms, and of course teaching with technology is no exception. The fact that the role of technology within the classroom is not consistent among educators is not in itself a bad thing: it is evidence of the kind of professional diligence that can protect our students from fads and flash-in-the-pan, reactive educational reforms. However, it is important that we take time to review our beliefs and make sure that any skepticism or reluctance to engage with emerging educational initiatives and approaches comes, as much as possible, from a place of professional objectivity and evidence.

Factors Contributing to Mindset

A wide range of factors (of which we as practitioners are not always consciously aware) influence our mindsets around technology, and these factors have the power to fundamentally affect whether and how we engage with technology in the classroom. Let's explore some of the background factors that play a role in creating and sustaining mindsets toward technology and start to evaluate whether these beliefs are helping or hindering the development of our teaching practices.

Context and Culture

Your context is essentially where you are in consideration of your surrounding circumstances. Your school context, for example, might be (but is not limited to)

- an early childhood, elementary, middle, or high school;

- a public, private, or parent-initiative school; and

- a rural, suburban, or urban school.

Culture can mean many things, from the big picture of societal culture, to more personal levels of culture, but it describes the ideas and social behavior within a setting. Your school culture could be

- collaborative;

- top-down;

- open to change; or

- authoritarian.

Teachers tend to be quite aware of school contextual factors, but there is rarely an opportunity for teachers to explore how culture in its more personal forms has influenced their mindset and practice and played a central role in defining who they are today, inside the classroom and out.

Technology is accessible to different extents in different parts of the world and carries differing degrees of significance in daily life. It is understandable that someone growing up today in Silicon Valley, for example, may take with them into adulthood a set of experiences

Questions to Think About

- **What value does your societal culture place on technology?**

- **What were your parents' views on technology (if indeed they had any and you know what they were)?**

- **If you are a parent now, what are your views about technology in your children's lives?**

- **In your social circle, how important is technology, and what is it used for?**

- **What do you personally use technology for outside of work: entertainment, creativity, communication, something else?**

- **If you had to choose three adjectives to describe the role technology plays in your culture and context outside of work, what would they be?**

- **If you are an avid or hesitant user of technology in your personal life, do you notice that being reflected in your classroom practice?**

in which technology has played a vastly different role than it has for someone living in a more rural or less tech-centric part of the world. In some societal cultures, outdoor, active time is more highly valued for children than indoor time, and in others it is the opposite. Culture also exists on smaller, more personal levels, such as the culture in your family as you were growing up and in your family now that you are the adult; the culture of your friendship groups; the culture of your school and school community; and the culture of any other part of your life in which you share space or ideas or beliefs with other people.

For example, our own cultural experiences have influenced our attitudes toward technology in life and education in subtle ways. Technology was an element of both of our lives growing up, and it was a part of the world around us, but it was certainly not very important to either of our lives. Our parents did not have (or at least didn't communicate) strong opinions about technology's role in our family lives, and we each had access to technology at home that was typical of the 1990s, such as a single PC that the family shared.

We were certainly exposed to far less technology, and as such fewer associated pressures, than young people are today. Sarah, for example, got her first mobile phone at the age of seventeen but faced none of the temptation or pressure that modern teenagers face (or that she as an adult now faces!), because texting the one other person she knew who had a phone and playing "Snake" were significantly less alluring than the options available on smartphones today. When we were growing up, technology was around us, but it was in moderate use and played only a minor role in our lives. Although our personal use of technology has increased as its availability and ease of use have increased, we are nowhere near as embedded in technological culture as many children and teenagers today.

Education

The role your own education has played and continues to play in shaping your mindset about technology can be thought of in three ways:

1. Your educational experiences as a student in school

2. The education you received to become a teacher

3. The continuing professional development that you undertake in an ongoing capacity as a teacher

School education

The role technology played in your education at school will depend on both the context and the culture you were a part of as a student but also *when* you were a student. To return to our personal experiences as an example of this, when we were high-school students in the mid-1990s, technology was treated as a subject completely divorced from other subjects in the school. Technology was used during "Computing," in which we learned (and instantly forgot) something about bits and bytes, and "Keyboard Skills," where we learned to type without looking at the keyboard while a teacher called out a string of letters.

If you went to school before that time, technology as we think of it today may have been totally absent from your experience as a student, or if you went later it may have played a larger role. However, the likelihood is that almost everyone reading this book will have one thing in common in terms of their experience of technology in school: if it was covered at all, it was almost certainly a stand-alone subject. For most it was a subject taught in a specific room, with a curriculum of its own, and physical technology was probably absent, or at least significantly less plentiful, in every other room or subject in the school than in the official computer room or lab.

In our experience, this has not changed in many schools to the degree that we believe it needs to in order to provide students with access to technology and learning experiences that match their needs beyond school. While we are in part a product of our prior experiences with technology in the classroom, we are now developing professionals who are creating, leading, and working within schools that have the potential to do more than perpetuate this isolated technology model that was a feature of school for many of us.

Teacher education

We both studied education in the early to mid-2000s, in different countries and very different educational systems. In spite of the geographical and cultural distance between our courses, the way they addressed technology teaching and learning was remarkably similar: they didn't. Neither of us was given practical training in how to use technology or pedagogical guidance on how we could use it in the classroom, in spite of the fact that there was a technology curriculum we would be expected to teach once we were qualified. There was also no deeper consideration of the purpose of technology in education or exploration of how technology might be used to enhance learning in other curricular areas.

Data published by the Organisation for Economic Co-operation and Development (OECD) in 2019 shows that in 2017 in the United States, 56 percent of public-school teachers were over forty, of which 29 percent were over fifty, and only 16 percent were under thirty. There are rare international examples where those numbers are reversed, such as in the United Kingdom, but in general the proportion of teachers over fifty is at around twice as high as those under thirty. This means that the majority of public-school teachers have had educational experiences, in school and during undergraduate and graduate training, in which technology was a minimal component of their education, if it was considered at all. These same teachers are, however, now expected to use and teach with technology in front of cohorts of students who are increasingly technologically capable and experienced. This theme of disparity is known as the "digital native versus the digital immigrant" theory. (See Figure 3.1.)

**Digital Natives Versus Digital Immigrants:
Definition and Impact**

	DIGITAL NATIVE	DIGITAL IMMIGRANT
DEFINITION	A person brought up during the digital age, who has therefore been familiar with digital technology and the Internet from childhood.	A person brought up before digital technology became widespread.
IMPACT	This means everyone we have been teaching for the last fifteen years at least, along with many of today's newly qualified teachers.	This means the majority of established teachers working within and leading schools today.

Figure 3.1

The main idea behind digital natives versus digital immigrants argues that comfort with technology is a purely generational phenomenon: if you were born in the digital era, you will be more comfortable with technology than if you were not. Contrasting research argues that there are other factors that matter just as much as age in determining a person's comfort level with technology:

- gender

- educational level

- experience

- to what degree the person uses technology in daily life

These theoretical arguments have real-world implications: if we believe that our ability to interact with technology is limited by our age, then we believe that ability cannot be improved, and research shows that it absolutely can (Helsper and Enyon 2010). When we describe or think of ourselves as digital immigrants, it encourages a fixed, deficit mindset around technology, permitting and reinforcing a self-image of a person who is bad with technology. In reality, our ability with technology is a product of our experiences, our beliefs, and our desire to use it. We are all capable of raising our skill and confidence level with technology. Being willing to take the risk and make the effort to do so is the kind of growth mindset we want to be modeling for our students.

Making a distinction between general comfort, confidence, and ability with technology in our personal lives and the way that we use it in the classroom is important. Many young teachers joining the profession within the last five years might be described as digital natives who are very comfortable with using technology in their day-to-day lives. However, younger teachers are not necessarily more able to use technology confidently and effectively than teachers who have been in the profession for longer *for the purpose of enhancing teaching and learning*. Unfortunately, many graduate education institutions and courses continue to focus on the what of technology, as opposed to the why or the how. In general, technology continues to be considered a stand-alone subject during undergraduate and postgraduate teacher education. Very few institutions take steps to make sure that student teachers are comfortable with actually using the technology they will be expected to teach with when they get into the classroom. More important, it is very rare to find courses or institutions where student teachers are asked to consider the purpose and role of technology in education and to develop a philosophy or mindset around its use.

That sense of purpose and vision about the deeper meaning and potential of technology in education matters a great deal. The teachers who use technology most effectively are not those who are the youngest or the most tech-savvy, but rather those who have a clear purpose and vision for the role of technology in their teaching and who are committed to learning what they need to learn to realize that vision.

At this point, please pause and think for a moment about what *you* believe technology's role in education is or should be, and even write it down so you can return to it later and see if it changes over time.

Questions to Think About

- How important was technology in your education when you were a student?

- Where and how was technology taught to you: was it stand-alone, integrated, skills-based, something else?

- In your training to become a teacher, how explicitly was technology addressed? Do you feel it prepared you to use technology when you entered the profession?

- Do you see any ways in which the beliefs and expectations about technology that were formed in your own educational experience continue to affect your thinking and practice today?

Professional Development

Although the universities taking a deliberate and thoughtful approach to technology education are still in the minority, they are on the increase, which is great news for new teachers entering the profession. But what about the tens of millions of teachers already in the profession globally?

Professional development (PD) is a core part of every teacher's working life. From weekend workshops and conferences, to online courses, to inservice training and staff meetings, there is an expectation that all teachers are lifelong learners. The priorities for that lifelong learning may be driven by personal interest, school needs, or the demands of the wider education system, so whether and how a teacher is asked to focus on developing their skills and understandings related to technology use, teaching and integration depends very much on context.

A wide body of research has shown that the effectiveness of PD in changing classroom practice for the better is dependent on it having the following characteristics (Whitehouse 2011):

- based on the needs of students and teachers

- sustained

- subject-specific

- rooted in classroom practice

- collaborative and reflective

- predicated on external expertise

Effective PD leads to meaningful, sustainable change. But if you consider the majority of technology PD you have received at your school, would you say it met those criteria?

One of the ways we see most teachers receiving training in technology is often through PD days, in which the school is closed for one or two days and the whole staff focuses on one aspect of school development. Common topics for these sessions when they focus on technology include SMART Board training, G Suite for Education (Google), or specific functions related to the attendance or reporting software the school uses, for example. Generally, they are stand-alone, undifferentiated, and highly skills-centric; they offer little to no opportunity to practice or make mistakes; and they lack discussion related to how the technology might affect what happens in the classroom.

Sometimes schools will take the professional development day model a step further, offering optional or differentiated technology workshops for teachers to sign up for based on their needs; however, while teachers generally perceive this as a definite improvement on the one-size-fits-all approach, it still fails to address all of the key indicators for effective PD.

We have yet to meet a teacher who attended sessions like these who felt it made a profound difference to his or her understanding and approach toward technology; on the contrary, ineffective technology training seems to contribute toward negative teacher mindset. For teachers to begin to think about technology as transformative, effective, enhancing, and exciting for students, it makes sense that the experiences they have with technology in their own learning need to mirror that. In the upcoming section in this chapter "Elements That Foster a Positive Institutional Technology Mindset" (page 28), we offer some suggestions for what more effective technology PD could look like.

Experience

When you have planned a lesson that relies heavily on technology, what do you typically worry about before the lesson? Is it student behavior? The weather? How engaged the students will be? Or is it whether the technology will fail on you at the last minute? For many teachers, the experiences we have had over our time in education have conditioned us to be fearful that the technology will fail when we need it most, and, let's be honest, it often does! The Wi-Fi drops out, or the projector bulb blows, or the PC just won't switch on—*again*—and the stress that it produces in teachers is often quite extreme. If you reflect on the physical feelings that you have had when this crisis has befallen you (and we are 100 percent sure that it has at some point), you might describe prickly heat, sweating, racing heart, irritation, embarrassment, and a host of other negative emotions. Years of unsuccessful experiences with technology often understandably lead teachers to give up entirely on the idea of integrating technology in their teaching.

But instead of asking, "Why do negative experiences with technology make teachers less inclined to use it?" we should ask, "How can we help teachers to view negative experiences with technology in the same way as we view other negative experiences in teaching?" and "How can we model for students the process of learning to deal effectively with the frustrations that technology can sometimes cause?"

Teachers frequently put enormous amounts of effort and time into innovative learning engagements that might be interrupted or ruined by a fire drill or any number of unexpected events. Our plans can be (and are!) often derailed by normal events of daily school life, but the majority of us are not so affected by these incidents that we refuse to go on field trips or plan unusual and exciting lessons.

The difference perhaps lies with teachers' comfort with failure under a variety of circumstances and how confident we feel thinking on our feet to change plans at the last second. For many teachers, when technology fails we feel we are left with no backup: we were reliant on the YouTube video, or the presentation, or the Wi-Fi connection to make the lesson work. In non-technology-related lessons, teachers will generally have considered alternatives, or will have the experience and confidence to adjust their plans in the moment to make their lesson fit the given situation, or will simply put the lesson aside until tomorrow and fill the gap with something else. For many teachers, however, when technology fails it is uniquely stressful, and uniquely memorable. If, in teachers' experience, technology has let them down routinely this is likely to cause a growing unwillingness to continue to try to use technology in the classroom. In our work with teachers we are often asked why we don't feel this stress or how we get technology to work for us reliably. The simple answers are that we *do* find it stressful when technology fails and we *don't* always get it to work, but we have a few strategies that really help to moderate that stress and keep the lesson going when all else fails, which we share with you in "Tips for Developing a Positive Classroom Mindset" (page 30).

When we think about negative experiences with technology, day-to-day classroom and work issues are what come to mind first for many teachers, but there are subtler, more pervasive components that, when *lacking*, contribute to creating and perpetuating a negative mindset around technology.

Support

Support can mean many things: it can mean practical training, responsive help when technology goes awry, a dedicated colleague whose job it is to support technology integration, the understanding and backing of colleagues and teammates, or the sense that school leadership places value on what is happening in teaching and learning.

Curriculum

The extent to which technology can be integrated depends to a large degree on how the written curriculum, both general (English, math, etc.) and technology-specific, is structured to allow this. A mainly skills-based, stand-alone technology curriculum will present challenges when you're trying to meaningfully integrate technology into the classroom. In contrast, a thoughtfully designed, integrated technology curriculum teaches transferable skills and enhances learning across the entire school curriculum. We discuss curriculum in more detail in Chapter 7.

Resources and infrastructure

Resources (explored in greater depth in Chapter 8) refer to the tangible, visible, accessible tools that teachers can use, such as robots, tablets, online subscriptions, apps, people, and even professional development. Infrastructure refers to the basic physical and organizational structures that your school needs to run. Sometimes these are visible—SMART Boards, printers, and photocopy machines—and sometimes they're hidden away, like the server or the operational budget, or they're intangible, like Wi-Fi. While we acknowledge that schools vary greatly around the world, in any school, whatever resources and infrastructure are available need to be stable. Integrating technology means using it as a tool to enhance learning across the curriculum, which ideally means technology needs to be in place in all classrooms, in sufficient quantities for students to use it as needed.

Purpose and vision

A lack of a defined, articulated, and shared school vision for technology can be a major factor in creating a lack of motivation to use it (we address this further in Chapter 9). Making the shift from teaching technology to integrating technology begins with an opportunity to have a conversation and develop understanding. You are not likely to achieve teacher engagement without a clear vision and purpose that teachers have access to, that they understand, and that a majority (or in the beginning, at least a strong minority) believe in.

We explore these areas in greater detail in the coming chapters and suggest strategies and approaches to address them in your context because we believe that for technology integration to be effective and truly enhance teaching and learning, a school community needs to plan for or develop all the pieces of the puzzle.

Elements That Foster a Positive Institutional Mindset

If reading this chapter has led you to reflect on your own mindset or the mindset of your staff, great! The first questions to ask yourself are, "Is the mindset more negative or positive?", "Why is that?", and "What can I do to shift it?"

Developing or changing an institutional mindset takes an investment of time, attention, and resources. How much time and attention, and which resources, will depend greatly on the current prevailing mindset and the individual needs of your school, but in general there are several elements that all schools need to address to some degree.

Purpose

What do you as a school believe about the role of technology in learning and in life? Many school leaders and many mission statements have a stated philosophy of using technology to enhance learning, but it takes effort to turn a deep understanding of what this means from words to reality.

Involving teachers in the process of exploring and defining purpose can be challenging, but it creates an opportunity to build shared understanding and vocabulary, explore your school community's current mindset, and build a vision that is shared from the outset by as many as possible.

Prioritization

Time is possibly every school leader's and teacher's most scarce resource: there are always so many elements of school development to address and there is only so much time. The fact is, not everything can be a priority, but technology can and should be integrated effectively in a way that supports most of the core development priorities a school has, such as assessment, differentiation, inclusion, literacy, or math. Prioritizing technology integration is the first and most important step in developing the positive mindset needed to make that shift.

If teachers are going to be expected to change what happens in the classroom, it's important that those changes are noticeably valued at the leadership level. That means

- devoting time and resources to effective training, discussion, and planning (see pedagogy section on page 30);

- actively encouraging and looking out for technology use and integration in staff observations, goal setting, and appraisal; and

- working to keep the topic of technology integration visible and valued by, for example, consistently highlighting and sharing good examples in staff emails, bulletins, and communication to parents.

Practical Support

For a positive technology mindset to develop on the institutional level, teachers need access to a range of practical support. Different schools will naturally vary in the ways they structure and allocate funding for this.

Technical support

Whom can teachers call when they have technology issues? How quickly will help arrive, and how friendly will it be when it gets there? If staff feel that they can't rely on support when they have a crisis, or that the help they do get will come with a side of criticism, judgment, or embarrassment, they are unlikely to feel positive about technology use.

Similarly, who will be responsible for managing the technology teachers will use? Having a dedicated, accessible, and approachable member of staff who is responsible for adding apps, ordering resources, and setting up devices means that teachers' requests are handled promptly, professionally, and effectively. This frees them up to think only about student need and learning, and it ensures they have what they need when they need it.

Pedagogical support

The most valuable technology resource for teachers is someone who can plan with them, model, coteach, or support them in their practice—combining technological expertise with an understanding of the wider curricula and approaches of the school. Consider how you could use human and financial resources flexibly to provide pedagogical support. That might mean hiring a full-time technology integrator or facilitator if you are in the fortunate position to be able to do so, restructuring an existing IT teaching role, supporting willing teachers to become tech coaches for their grade level, or reaching out to other schools to create links and relationships and share pedagogical support.

Professional development

While one-off training sessions can be helpful, in our experience, the most valuable and effective professional development comes from sustained, contextual, in-house training, discussion, and development, led by staff with relevant expertise that is directly linked to the school's context and needs. In-house professional development could take the form of professional learning communities, one-to-one or small-group differentiated training, or a sustained series of staff meetings around a topic or set of connected topics. This provides an opportunity to deliver highly differentiated, contextualized professional development that can be sustained and can evolve over time according to changing needs. It also allows for ongoing follow-up and reflection.

Schools can use such professional development not only to build teacher capacity and confidence but also to provide a forum for continued discussion and development around purpose and vision.

Pedagogy

Almost all schools have some form of technology curriculum in place, but it is vital to undertake a deliberate review of how (or whether) the school's existing technology curriculum, scope and sequence, or classroom learning objectives align with your purpose and vision. Building a thoughtful integrated technology curriculum provides teachers with a clearly articulated framework for integrating technology meaningfully into teaching and learning.

How that curriculum comes to life is dependent on effective planning, scaffolding, and instruction with and for technology. These are core skills teachers can continuously improve, reflect upon, and apply to their practice with support and guidance.

Physical infrastructure and resources

Physical infrastructure and resources should support the school's purpose and vision for technology integration, meet the needs of students and teachers, and be built on a pedagogical foundation. That means that the systems, teacher tools, and teaching tools should be planned and developed to facilitate the curriculum and—where possible—decisions about future infrastructural development should be made in collaboration with the teachers who will be using it in their classrooms, with an understanding and appreciation of the school's technology vision.

Tips for Developing a Positive Classroom Mindset

When technology fails, it doesn't have to spell disaster. We can learn to take these issues in stride and keep the bigger picture in mind to maintain a positive technology mindset, though admittedly this is definitely not easy. Following are a few tips to keep technology failures in your control.

Take a Deep Breath and Stay Calm

When technology fails, teachers often feel one of the following emotions:

- *Anxiety*: We feel responsible and are afraid we have probably broken something expensive and difficult to fix; we are worried we will lose control of the students or lesson because of the interruption.

- *Annoyance*: We believe the technology is annoying and is responsible for ruining the lesson.

- *Embarrassment*: We worry the students will judge and laugh at us for having problems with the technology.

As we said before, we also feel these things when our lessons (with or without technology) go wrong—these are natural responses to stress. To get back on track, *take a deep breath*—staying calm in the moment will let you think creatively and work around the problem so your students can keep learning. Once the crisis has passed, give yourself space to *consider why technology failure feels so stressful to you*. Is it the fear of looking silly in front of the students? Is it fear of not knowing how to solve the problem yourself? If you feel differently when your lesson is derailed by technology than you do when it is derailed by all the other things that don't go according to plan in the school day, why is that? Taking that step back from the negative feelings technology might provoke in you in difficult moments can give you a great deal of control over your own reaction and help you to respond more effectively, as well as help you to be more conscious and objective about your own mindset and the driving forces behind it.

Over time you will *develop personal resilience* for the situations when technology lets you down.

Try Not to Overgeneralize

It might not *feel* like it, but in most parts of the developed world, the Internet and the technology in the school probably work vastly more often than not. If you take a step back and look objectively at how often the technology has failed you, we hope you will find the instances, while likely highly memorable, were in the minority.

This may not be the case, of course, if you teach in a part of the world with infrastructure that has been fundamentally damaged by war or poverty or in which the infrastructure is not yet fully developed because either it is very rural or funding is particularly lacking. In cases like these it is important to plan to use technology in a way that is realistic and as reliable as possible. If you really cannot rely on the Internet or your devices to work from one lesson to the next, let alone one day to the next, for example, it is understandable that you will not be keen to invest your limited time in planning lessons that are as likely or more likely to fail as to work. In these cases, think about what you could do to work around the issue, for example, by downloading videos in advance if this is a possibility for you. If your school has funding for technology but your country or area has poor infrastructure, you could look into what technology resources could be put in place that do not rely on the Internet (e.g., offline software and apps).

Involve Your Students

As galling as it may be to receive technical support from a six-year-old, your students may well be able to help you with whatever is going wrong. Why is it that a child can so easily handle the kinds of technology issues we adults find so challenging? One school of thought would favor the theory about digital natives versus digital immigrants that we touched on earlier; however, we are inclined to believe it really comes down to growth versus fixed mindsets and a lack of fear. Students do not generally think of themselves in the restrictive terms a fixed mindset reinforces, as being "techy" or "technologically challenged." They aren't afraid to push buttons or try things and see or to google the issue and have a go at implementing the suggestions they find. In general, children have very little fear of breaking technology, so they demonstrate a level of personal entrepreneurship and self-reliance that allows them to solve problems easily. The good news is that they are right to feel so little fear of breaking things: breaking modern technology by pushing buttons and clicking things is almost impossible, so let your students help you and you can all learn together! If you have students who are very tech-savvy or who would benefit from the extra responsibility, why not give them the role of tech support in your classroom? They will quickly become familiar with the most common issues that come up and will revel in the opportunity to help and become experts.

Be Honest About What Went Wrong

Sometimes technology just fails. Road workers cut the Internet cable in the street, or the school server updates in the middle of the school day, or your PC just dies for no reason. While it is important to have an awareness of the potential for technology to fail so you can be prepared to deal with it when it happens, this is different from the attitude that says, "There's no point trying; it never works anyway." The likelihood is that it works more often than it fails, but those moments when it fails and you don't know what to do tend to stick in your mind!

Sometimes, though, lessons featuring technology fail because we didn't test our idea out and make sure it would work or that it would work in the way we imagined. Often schools have firewalls or protocols running behind the scenes that block access to certain websites or prevent tools from working the way they would in your house. If the lesson failed because of something totally outside your control, then that really is annoying! If the technical failure could perhaps have been avoided by better or different preparation, or some other factor in your control, it is best to reflect on that and think about what you could do differently next time—it happens to everyone at some point, and not just when using technology!

Stay Focused on the Learning Objective

As we discuss in the coming chapters, the purposeful integration of technology is always rooted in student learning. If the technology fails, come back to the learning objective: what was the purpose of the lesson? It wasn't to make an iMovie, or watch a YouTube clip, or even code a robot, but rather to develop communication skills, brainstorm character traits, or follow multistep directions. Keeping the learning objective right at the forefront of your thinking means that even if the tool or resource you were planning to use lets you down at the last minute, you can always go low-tech, address it some other way, and return to your technology integration another day.

Build Capacity

For school leaders or teachers looking to develop confidence with technology, capacity building is incredibly important. For more detail, see Chapter 9, but in general we recommend breaking technology capacity building down into two main areas: teaching tools and teacher tools (see Figure 3.2).

Technology-focused professional development for teachers often centers on teaching tools. This makes sense in many ways; after all, teaching and learning is what it is all about, and schools and teachers want to improve practice in the areas they believe will have the greatest direct impact on student learning. However, for most teachers new to integration or hesitant about technology, it makes sense to begin building capacity in the areas that affect them most in their day-to-day work, and that means providing PD opportunities in teacher tools. There is often an assumption that because desktops have been in common use in business and education since the mid-1990s, teachers are confident and comfortable using them. But this is often not the case. Struggling every day to use technology that is integral to your work will have a predictably negative impact on your mindset and willingness to take risks with integrating teaching tools.

Teaching Tools and Teacher Tools:
Tools for Building Capacity

TEACHING TOOLS

Teaching tools are the technologies we use with students in the classroom to enhance their learning. In different schools that will mean different things, and the incredibly rapid rate of development in technology means that any list including specific hardware or software is likely to become out-of-date very quickly!

For example:

- desktop computers or tablets
- robots
- digital toys
- apps
- software used by students
- digital displays
- interactive whiteboards
- sound systems within the classroom

TEACHER TOOLS

Teacher tools, on the other hand, are the technologies teachers have to use to do their jobs beyond the classroom. There is a continual increase in the level of communication, collaboration, and engagement with technology on a daily basis within a school community.

For example:

- desktop computers
- email
- word-processing software
- attendance and grading software
- planning software
- cloud-based storage

Figure 3.2

Move Forward with a Positive Technology Mindset

We have tried to frame some of the factors that have an impact on individual mindsets around technology, both professionally and personally. Taking a step back from past personal experiences and considering how they might influence how we behave, what we believe, and how we teach in the present is the first step to developing a more positive mindset around technology. Challenging our assumptions, biases, beliefs, and actions about technology is a central part of being a reflective practitioner, and it can only make our teaching more intentional.

For technology integration to truly enrich the learning within the classroom, a positive technology mindset is vital.

1. Identify and confront your current mindset.

2. Recognize areas of your mindset that are negatively affecting your practice.

3. Take action to address those areas.

You will then be on your way to making significant developments in how technology is integrated in your classroom and school. With these developments in place, you'll be able to better prepare your students for a rapidly changing and increasingly technological world and harness technology's unique potential to enhance and enrich learning to benefit your students.

Reflection

- *If your goal is supporting student learning:* How do you feel about the role of technology in the lives of students in and out of school and in your own life? Do your personal feelings about technology have an impact on how and how much you use it in your classroom?

- *If your goal is supporting professional learning:* What support do teachers really need to feel more positive about technology in the classroom on a day-to-day basis? How can you open a dialogue with teachers about their technology mindsets and the factors influencing them?

- *If your goal is supporting curriculum development:* Are your curriculum documents structured in a way that enables, supports, or hinders technology integration?

- *If your goal is supporting organizational systems and structures:* What elements of technology infrastructure are most frustrating or difficult for teachers? Reliability, access, quantity, ease of use? What can you do in the short, medium, and long term to build or develop technical systems, structures, and resources to facilitate technology use and integration?

Pedagogy

04

Enhancing Student Communication

O ur students face a host of communication challenges in the modern classroom. How can an academically capable eighth-grade student who understands a concept or who has mastered a skill, but is new to English, demonstrate their knowledge and engage in classroom learning? How can a first-grade emergent writer who is an excellent storyteller share their stories effectively with others? How can our students communicate conceptual, complex, and creative ideas in ways that meet their learning needs and that match the purpose of the learning? And, finally, how can one adult support all of this in a way that is both manageable and sustainable?

Reflecting, participating, sharing ideas, demonstrating learning, asking questions—the list of ways in which students communicate for and about learning is very long. It is, after all, one of the core elements of learning in any classroom! We could categorize approaches and purposes for student communication in a number of ways, but we have co-opted and adapted the structure of Keene and Zimmerman's (1997) well-known text comprehension strategy of making connections to break down student classroom communication into three categories:

1. *Student to self:* reflection on their own learning

2. *Student to other:* communication with peers or teachers within their school

3. *Student to world:* communication with others beyond the school, public sharing, or publishing of work with the wider world

Challenges and Solutions, Digital Approaches and Tools

The challenges we face in the classroom in supporting our students with communication are constant, but the technology approaches and tools that are available to us to provide the solutions to those challenges are changing all the time. To be sure of providing you with the most up-to-date information possible to support you in choosing the best digital tools for the job, we have created online resources that we can easily and regularly update as approaches and tools change over time. In this chapter and Chapter 5, after each set of challenges and solutions, you will find links to these online resources, which are available on the Heinemann website at Hein.pub/Tech-Resources.

First, let's look at common classroom activities within each category and explore why and how technology can support and enhance student communication for learning.

Student to Self

One major application of student-to-self communication in learning is the process of reflection. Reflection is becoming an increasingly common and valued element of formative assessment and self-assessment, but why do we ask our students to reflect?

Illustrating Integration: Ali and Jo

Ali and Jo are fourth-grade students who are doing gymnastics in their physical education class. Every week, Ali, Jo, and their classmates practice the skills they have learned, and the teacher demonstrates a

new skill, which the students then practice in pairs. Over the weeks, the pairs work together to create a routine of their own, demonstrating the skills they have learned in a sequence. Ms. Banks, the sports teacher, has set up a recording station in one corner of the gym, and each week the pairs of students visit the station and record their routines onto their digital learning journals. The students must review their videos after recording. They immediately spot where their technique needs some extra work during that class, and they can watch all of their videos back and see how their technique and routine have improved over the previous weeks. Because they have the resources and time to record and review their own performance, Ali and Jo can continuously reflect, self-assess, and make improvements to the skills they are learning.

Reflection is not only about finding meaning from prior learning experiences but also about using higher-order thinking skills to make connections between different activities, successes, challenges, subjects, and disciplines.

Implementing and facilitating reflection for students so that it is meaningful for them *and* manageable for the teacher is not always easy. For many teachers, time pressure and the demands of a diverse or high-needs class may crowd out reflection or limit its effectiveness. However, by teaching our students strategies to encourage and support reflective thinking, we help them develop the ability to apply new knowledge, understanding, and skills to their wider learning.

Reflection is a highly individualized process; it is about students taking time to reflect on their own learning, their own needs and challenges, and their own strengths. For teachers, the challenge lies in finding realistic and sustainable strategies and approaches that allow students to undertake an abstract process in a practical way.

Effective Reflection Requirements

To reflect effectively, students need the following:

- the opportunity to reflect *frequently* and *repeatedly* throughout the learning process

- guidance in using *critical thinking* and *questioning* skills

- access to relevant and recent learning *examples* and *prompts*

- an emphasis on reflecting on *process* rather than *product*

If the mechanism for reflecting is manageable and accessible for students, this frees up the time and attention they need to focus on the true purpose of reflection: deep, critical thinking.

Strategies and Tools to Support Reflection

A powerful tool for promoting effective student reflection is the digital learning journal. Many schools use student portfolios, which traditionally have been a collection of examples of best work kept in physical portfolios or binders. It can be challenging to reflect on the work in these physical portfolios, however (often forcing teachers to hand out slips of paper with smiley faces or short comments on them), and they are best designed for *storing products*, not *communicating process*.

Students benefit most from reflecting on the process of their learning; after all, they are not likely to need to do another essay, painting, or math test identical to the one they have done. But they will need to write a *different* essay, paint *another* picture, or do a math test on a *different* topic. Reflecting on a single product is not as helpful to their future learning as reflecting on the difficulties and successes they faced in the process they went through to create that product.

Digital learning journals are specifically designed to enable students to record and communicate the *process* of learning and to communicate beyond what can be captured on paper and they can be used across the curriculum with any age of student. The ability to add photos and videos of ongoing learning or hands-on learning engagements, as well as to upload finished digital products, photos of summative tasks, and completed assignments, means that students can not only communicate more richly but also have accessible and meaningful prompts to refer to in reflection. Some digital learning journal software also has the option for students to add audio comments rather than only text, simplifying the process of reflection for students for whom writing may create barriers, such as early readers and writers, English language learners, and students with learning difficulties.

This, of course, does not mean that paper portfolios have no place in the classroom: sometimes they are the very best way to store a piece of work and therefore to enable reflection at a later date. The decision to keep paper portfolios in addition to digital portfolios depends very much on *purpose*: what platforms will best support your aims as a teacher and the needs of your students?

There are many high-quality digital learning journal platforms to choose from but remember that software lacks the permanence and tangibility of paper portfolios. It is wise to opt for software that has the option to roll over content at the end of the year to promote continuity and that also allows you, the student, or family members to download or export the digital learning journal at the end of each year in case the software is discontinued.

Enhancing Student-to-Self Communication with Technology: Challenges and Solutions

CHALLENGES	SOLUTIONS
→ Teachers need an easy way to enable students to reflect on both the process and the products of learning.	→ Digital learning journals provide a student-friendly platform on which to record, store, and reflect on work, and they allow students and teachers to easily access and review historical work.
→ Creating and managing opportunities for students to reflect frequently throughout the learning process is difficult on paper.	→ Digital learning journals often allow for text and audio commenting on items by teachers and students, and they enable teachers and students to record the process of learning through videos and photos.
→ Teachers need to support students in making explicit links between past, present, and future learning experiences.	→ Digital note-taking tools allow students to make and share notes on learning more seamlessly and in ways that match their learning needs. They can record their thinking process for future reflection.
→ Supporting students to record and externalize their thinking in ways that are accessible and that support rather than distract from the reflection process can be difficult.	

To access the regularly updated online resources with more detailed challenges and solutions plus digital approaches and tools, either scan the QR code on page ix or visit Hein.pub/Tech-Resources.

Note-taking is often most closely associated with research, but it can also support the process of reflection. Creating mind maps and taking notes during learning can reveal the students' meaning-making process, what aspects of the content are most important to them, and how they organize their thoughts.

In your classroom, how and when might your students benefit from having the option to reflect in different ways? When might they benefit from being able to revisit concrete examples of their learning in service of reflection? The following examples might give you some ideas:

- *Math*: After recording themselves solving a mathematical problem and explaining aloud the strategies they are using to solve it, students can reflect on whether the process was correct or incorrect and how they have developed their skill and understanding. They can refer back to that thought process when solving similar problems or working with related concepts in the future.

- *Reading aloud*: By listening to audio recordings of themselves reading aloud, students can reflect on their tone, expression, and fluency and hear real progress over time.

- *Group-work skills*: By reviewing a video of their group working on a problem, students can observe their own behavior and role in the group and examine how the group collaborated. Later, they can reflect on the group's strengths and areas for improvement.

Student to Other

We constantly ask our students to communicate with others for different purposes throughout the school day. Student communication includes presenting their learning, participating, discussing and debating, questioning, sharing ideas, and offering and receiving constructive criticism.

Presenting

For teachers to find out whether their students have learned and understood what was intended, and for students to have an opportunity to demonstrate their learning, summative presentation tasks are an invaluable tool.

Illustrating Integration: Lisa

Lisa is an eighth-grade student who has been studying World War II in her history and social science class. Throughout the term she has learned about the economic, military, and social factors that precipitated the war and the long-term social and political effects it caused. To demonstrate her learning, Lisa had the choice to either write a traditional essay or create a product showing her knowledge using technology. Lisa felt that adequately communicating the complexity of the interrelated factors and the reality of the war would be most suited to audiovisual media. So she elected to create a short movie combining contemporary photographs and archival video footage, simple animations to show the movement of military forces and human populations, and an informative voice-over. With this, she was able to provide a richer, more multidimensional picture not only of the topic but of her understanding of the concepts that would transfer to her learning about other conflicts over time.

In the vignette about Lisa, we looked at one of the most common formal aspects of student-to-other communication: presenting learned knowledge or understanding. Effective technology integration can give students the option to communicate that learning in whatever way allows them to express themselves most clearly. In Lisa's case, technology gave her the option to communicate her learning audiovisually, adding depth and detail to her communication. Where those opportunities exist in your classroom will depend on the subject and the age group you teach. In general, many big concepts and ideas, physical processes, and topics with complex and interdependent factors lend themselves better to a multimedia approach to communication than to essays and written reports.

Another way in which teachers often ask students to communicate their learning is through a formal oral presentation. It is increasingly common for the speech to be accompanied or illustrated by a digital presentation, and it is a somewhat unfair fact that often digital presentations are used as an example of lowest-common-denominator technology teaching and learning. The well-known SAMR model (Puentedura 2006), describes a hierarchy of technology's purpose in learning. It starts with *Substitution* on the bottom where technology "acts as a direct tool substitute, with no functional change", up through *Augmentation* ("Tech acts as a direct tool substitute, with functional improvement"), *Modification* ("Tech allows for significant task redesign"), and culminates in *Redefinition* where it says, "tech allows for the creation of new tasks, previously inconceivable". Within the SAMR model, digital presentations would be an example of Substitution or Augmentation, and the implication is that they are therefore a somewhat uninspired use of technology. In reality, it depends very much on the quality of the digital presentation skills that students learn and the underlying purpose for using a digital presentation as an aid to oral presentation. If teachers teach digital presentation with an emphasis on enhancing or illustrating speech, design principles, and visual literacy, then it can be a very meaningful and useful skill for students to learn and build on. After all, most skilled jobs involve an element of professional presentation!

As valuable as they are, for many students, oral presentations are highly stressful, and students for whom English is an additional language or who have learning difficulties may struggle to accurately communicate the depth of their understanding in an on-the-spot presentation format. You can assess many of the core presentation skills, such as appreciation of tone, word choice, audience, expression, and structure, by allowing students to record presentations and submit them digitally. Whether they simply give a speech alone to the camera or incorporate more elaborate approaches with animation or visual aids, this activity has a number of benefits for students and teachers:

- Students can watch their recordings back and improve them.

  › When students receive direct and meaningful feedback on their performance, they are usually more than happy to record their speech over and over again to improve it.

  › For students who are English language learners, hearing their own accent, pronunciation, and syntax will give them the time to identify where further work is needed and the opportunity to practice and improve.

  › Apps and software designed to incorporate images, animations, and videos can enhance student presentations even further.

- Teachers avoid the inherent management challenges of traditional student presentations.

  › Traditional in-class presentations absorb an enormous amount of class time, and this can create real issues with behavior management, student boredom, and lost learning time.

  › There is no opportunity for teachers to review traditional student presentations. After watching twenty or thirty speeches back-to-back or over a series of days, it would be beneficial to be able to look back and reconsider grades, compare different examples, or moderate across classes and students. Digital presentations offers teachers the chance to review different presentations and compare them.

You should always base your decision about the format for an oral presentation (in front of an audience versus digitally created) on purpose. What is the purpose of the presentation? Is it to practice presenting under stress, in front of a large group of people? Or is it simply to communicate learning and demonstrate effective word choice, tone, and structure? Being clear about the purpose helps you as a teacher to choose a method and medium for student presentations that is the most beneficial to the students and that takes advantage of the most useful tools and approaches for that purpose.

Participating, Discussing, and Questioning

Technology can be a helpful tool in creating a safe, controlled space for students to participate in class discussions and ask questions. Sometimes, having the option to ask a question or give an answer anonymously can give otherwise shy or disengaged students the confidence to participate. Various apps and software capitalize on this by allowing teachers to pose questions to gather student feedback or assess knowledge in a way that provides different levels of anonymity depending on what the teacher feels is appropriate.

Teachers can also use technology to great effect in facilitating how students communicate with each other in small-group settings such as guided reading groups and literature circles, discussion groups, and project groups. These settings require students to share thoughts and ideas as well as to record group learning and progress. Paper-based methods for recording and communicating those conversations and group learning experiences can make it difficult for teachers to access that learning in a real-time way. Collaborative apps and programs can be very helpful tools in gathering group communication by providing a central, shared space that is easily accessible for students and teachers. These tools become especially powerful during projects and activities where students are connecting learning between different classes and teachers. We look in greater detail at how technology can enhance the second of the three Cs, collaboration, in Chapter 5.

Illustrating Integration: Katarina

Katarina is a seventh-grade student who recently moved from the Czech Republic and is completely new to English. Katarina is a very capable student who was successful in her previous school, but in her new school she is struggling to demonstrate her knowledge and participate in her classes. In science, for example, the class is learning about photosynthesis. Katarina studied this already at her previous school, but her level of English prevents her from taking part in class discussions, working through the textbook, or answering written questions. As a result, she feels bored, disconnected, and isolated. Her teacher, Mr. Li, notices that Katarina is unhappy and decides to use technology to help her to participate in the class. First, he uses a translation program to help him communicate with Katarina. The program works on smartphones, tablets, and computers and translates his spoken English directly into Katarina's language. He explains that he wants her to create a product for him explaining everything she knows about the topic of photosynthesis, without using words, during class time. He suggests a number of apps and shows Katarina the basics of how to use them, and for the next three weeks, she works independently to learn how to use the apps and create her own visual product to communicate her knowledge. She uses the Internet and class resources to help her and she is exposed to the English vocabulary for the topic as she works. At the end, not only does Mr. Li have an assessment piece that allows him to see what Katarina knows and what she still needs to learn, but Katarina is able to participate in the topic at the same time as her peers, albeit in a different way. As a result she learns useful vocabulary, feels less isolated and more involved, and feels that her prior learning and knowledge level are being seen and valued. This makes it easier for Mr. Li to differentiate for her and bring her into future topics using the tools she is familiar with while her English level increases.

For students with differing language- or learning-based needs, technology can be the key that opens the door to being a part of the class and engaging with learning in a way that would be closed to them otherwise. Dyslexia, dysgraphia, and English language needs may prevent students from understanding verbal input and discussion, accessing written learning materials, and sufficiently communicating their own knowledge and understanding. Whether students have significant prior knowledge, like Katarina, or are completely new to a topic, learning and language barriers can be isolating in the classroom and often cause these students to disengage from the learning process.

Luckily, there is a wide range of assistive and adaptive programs designed to help students to participate.

- Translation tools have developed to the point that even free apps and software like Google Translate can instantly translate printed text using the device's camera or translate speech from one language to another in real time, in either text or spoken form.

- Text-to-speech apps allow students to use a tablet to quickly scan printed text and listen to it being read aloud, and speech-to-text apps allow students to dictate their work and accurately turn it into text.

- Excellent keyboard apps have been designed for students with dyslexia to help with spelling, grammar, and word choice, and there is even a font that is specifically designed to make it easier for students with dyslexia to read printed text.

Combining these specialist programs with the tools and approaches we introduced in the section on presentations allows all students to participate, communicate, and engage in learning in ways that would not otherwise be possible.

Giving and Receiving Feedback

Many of the tools and approaches we explored in relation to reflection for student-to-self communication have built-in functionality to support students and teachers in giving feedback through comments. From a practical perspective, the ability to have a permanent record of feedback on learning activities and engagements that would not normally have such a record, such as in the expressive arts, sports, and performance-based activities, is helpful for students, parents, teachers, and administrators. Students can refer back to comments they and their teachers have given as part of their reflection process, and teachers can use them to inform assessment, planning, and transition. Digital feedback also opens up a world of possibility in what and how teachers and students discuss and improve learning: audio comments for emergent readers and writers or students with learning difficulties and video comments to demonstrate a different way of doing an activity or solving a problem can make feedback much more meaningful for students who might otherwise struggle to understand it.

Apps and software designed to make everyday feedback (in the form of quizzes, exit tickets, and tests) more streamlined and immediate free up teachers to focus their energies on designing creative, challenging, and targeted assessment activities and create opportunities for teachers to build students' digital citizenship skills, which we will look at in more detail in the next section, "Student to World."

Enhancing Student-to-Other Communication with Technology: Challenges and Solutions

PRESENTING	
CHALLENGES	**SOLUTIONS**
→ Students' capacity to demonstrate and communicate knowledge and understanding through formal written summative tasks is highly dependent on writing ability.	→ Digital presentation tools allow students to communicate ideas and learning using multiple forms of media, matching medium to purpose.
→ Formal oral presentations are time-consuming for teachers and students to watch in real time and stressful for students with language or social difficulties.	→ Digital presentation products can be viewed and reviewed by teachers and students. This avoids excessive lost learning time and facilitates student reflection.
→ Some topics and concepts are difficult to adequately communicate through traditional written and oral methods.	

PARTICIPATION AND FEEDBACK

CHALLENGES	SOLUTIONS
→ Language and writing and reading difficulties present barriers to classroom participation for English language learners and students with learning difficulties or differing needs.	→ Adaptive and assistive technologies make learning materials accessible to students, facilitate two-way communication, and support students in participating in day-to-day learning.
→ Gathering feedback from students for formative assessment and to inform future planning can be time-consuming and difficult to manage practically.	→ Teachers can use apps and software to streamline and increase the efficiency of the process of gathering student feedback.
→ Managing group collaboration and communication so that teachers and students have access to ongoing group work and feedback is challenging, particularly during cross-curricular or transdisciplinary project work.	→ Collaborative learning apps and software store student work and teacher feedback in a cloud-based platform, meaning multiple students and teachers can access and edit it simultaneously.

To access the regularly updated online resources with more detailed challenges and solutions plus digital approaches and tools, either scan the QR code on page ix or visit Hein.pub/Tech-Resources.

Student to World

Effective learning relies on students making connections between what happens in the classroom and what happens in the world beyond. In student-to-world communication, students gather information from firsthand sources, share their ideas, and learn to communicate with a wide or unfamiliar audience in a safe, supported way.

Publishing and Sharing Student Ideas and Learning

For students, the process of sharing and publishing their ideas and work to a real-world audience can be highly motivating and provide relevance and context to in-class activities and learning. Publishing can take many forms, from blogs to websites, books to social media. The important element they all share is that they make student work accessible to an audience, and publishing is most meaningful to students when that audience is authentic and when they can receive real, constructive feedback from that audience.

Illustrating Integration: Class Website

Mr. Hannigan's fifth-grade class has been learning about tone and audience in nonfiction writing. In the past he has had his students write letters to adults outside the school, but the students never found the activity as engaging or as helpful as he he'd hoped. To address this, Mr. Hannigan has decided to build a class website that his students will update and maintain throughout the year. After gaining approval for the plan from his principal and checking what security and media-release measures he needs to take, he builds a simple, free website that he can make either public or accessible only to invited email addresses. He creates groups in his class based on interest, with each group taking responsibility for managing an area of the site: weekly blog updates, pictures of learning, announcements, homework, and so on. Before the groups start working on the site, Mr. Hannigan gives a series of minilessons on tone, audience, and the importance *of checking spelling, grammar, and punctuation, and he continues to extend these lessons as the year goes on. Because the students know their work will be seen by their parents, the rest of the class, and the school community, they are more motivated to produce high-quality work. Once the website is up and running and the weekly routines are in place to maintain it, Mr. Hannigan decides it is time to enable commenting on the site. The class works together to establish shared expectations about appropriate comments, which students then share with their parents. Now, when parents and students sign in to the website they can comment on the content. Mr. Hannigan moderates comments before publishing them and sometimes comes across a comment that doesn't meet their shared expectations. He uses these comments as a basis for ongoing discussion about digital citizenship and the importance of communicating online as respectfully and responsibly as we do in real life.*

Blogging has been a part of many teachers' and classes' routines for some years now, but it is worth restating just how motivating the process of writing for a real-world, large audience can be for students. In the vignette we used a closed class website as an example, but depending on the age of your students and the specific rules in your school, there are many other online publishing and communication avenues to explore.

Social media

Twitter scares some teachers and schools because it is not as easy to restrict and control as some other social media platforms: anyone can follow anyone, and this can open up the potential for students to be exposed to inappropriate language or content. However, students who are old enough to have their own Twitter accounts or teachers who have the blessing of their school to create a class or teacher Twitter account can reduce this risk by making sensible choices about whom they follow. Taking control of teaching students how to use a platform like Twitter safely and responsibly in spite of these concerns can help them to learn important real-world lessons in a safer, more supported way than they are likely to encounter if we don't address the issue in the classroom. Beyond these concerns, Twitter can be a particularly rewarding tool when teachers and students use it to share classroom learning, follow education hashtags, and connect with other teachers and classes to create their own personal learning network (PLN).

Ebooks and multimedia books

Publishing a book has never been more accessible: students can easily work individually or collaboratively to create and publish their own ebooks with text and multimedia content. At the more professional end of the spectrum are dedicated digital publishing platforms, like iBooks Author and Kindle Desktop Publishing, that will allow students to share and sell their books online, but students can also use Pages, Google Docs, Book Creator, or classroom tools and publish their products on a school or class website or digital learning journal.

Email

These days almost everyone is online, and being able to contact almost anyone, from your mother to Queen Elizabeth II, is just a question of knowing his or her email address. Now, we aren't suggesting your students should email the queen (or your mother) but, instead of writing book reports for their teacher or even the library, for example, students can email the authors of books they have read in class to share their feedback. Learning how to compose and write polite, comprehensible, and appropriate emails to adults under the supervision of a teacher is an excellent way to learn about and practice tone, word choice, and other important communication skills in context.

Video conferencing

Just as with email, many people can be contacted directly through video conferencing software such as Skype or Zoom, and experts are often more willing than you might imagine to make contact with students around the world. Video conferencing can allow students the opportunity to learn to communicate ideas and opinions or ask questions of a safe but unfamiliar adult, requiring them to use an appropriate tone and vocabulary while gaining valuable firsthand information from an expert in a relevant field.

Communicating Safely, Responsibly, and Respectfully

One of the challenges many teachers face with regard to student digital communication is knowing how to address the problems that arise from students' use of social media outside of school. Cyberbullying and inappropriate online interactions that take place when students are not at school nevertheless have an impact on classroom relationships, learning, and student welfare. But teachers have very little power to affect what students do in their own time, with their own devices.

Enhancing Student-to-World Communication with Technology: Challenges and Solutions

CHALLENGES	SOLUTIONS
⇀ Nondigital communication does not provide students with opportunities to learn and apply digital citizenship skills in safe, real-world contexts.	⇀ Allowing students to publish work through blogs, websites, or ebooks provides them with the experience of writing for large audiences, using appropriate tone, language, and style for the purpose.
⇀ When sharing print communication, students often have access only to local audiences rather than global experts and peers.	⇀ Connecting students with experts and other students globally through telecommunications software and collaborative platforms provides them with primary source information for research; gives them opportunities to develop perspective, empathy, open-mindedness, and international-mindedness; and allows them to practice safe and responsible online communication skills.
⇀ Providing students with authentic audiences with which to share learning is sometimes difficult to manage with print documents.	

To access the regularly updated online resources with more detailed challenges and solutions plus digital approaches and tools, either scan the QR code on page ix or visit Hein.pub/Tech-Resources.

What we *can* do is create opportunities for students to practice safe, responsible, and respectful online behaviors when they are in the classroom and make explicit links to how and why they should use those behaviors in the real world. Digital learning journals are an example of a safe, controlled environment in which to teach students to comment respectfully and effectively on digital content. Many platforms also share features with social media, such as liking, sharing, and commenting, which gives teachers the opportunity to create explicit links between classroom behaviors and social media behaviors.

The more access students have to technology that allows them to communicate with people around the world, the greater the educational focus on teaching them to be responsible digital citizens becomes. Our students need to learn what information and ideas to share as well as when and how to share them online in a safe way, and they must learn how to comment respectfully on the ideas and words of others. However, we are reaching the point (or perhaps we have long since overtaken it) when it will stop being helpful to talk about digital citizenship, and we should simply be talking about citizenship.

The availability of devices to students is increasing rapidly, with more and more classrooms, schools, and districts moving to a one-to-one model in which students are using devices like laptops and tablets during the entire school day, in every subject. In cases like that, talking about the skills students need to communicate respectfully, responsibly, and safely online as digital citizenship creates an expectation for teachers and students that these behaviors are specific to technology use, when in fact they are just how we should behave toward one another at all times, online and offline. We as teachers need to be aware of the potential for students to make poor choices in their use of technology, actively anticipate and address those choices, and express our expectations for technology use clearly. Digital citizenship is often seen as the responsibility of the technology coach or IT teacher, but when students and teachers are integrating technology across the curriculum, teaching citizenship (digital or otherwise) has to be everyone's duty.

Next Steps

In this chapter we have given you a variety of examples of ways in which technology could be used to enhance communication for different purposes and at different audience levels. As you know, we advocate a purpose-based approach to technology integration, which means it should meet a need and enhance student learning. Turn your thoughts to your own students and context. When and why do your students struggle to communicate ideas, understanding, or learning? In an ideal world, how would you wish to support them to communicate more effectively? Do you have access to technology that could help you achieve that ideal-world scenario?

This is how technology integration really begins, so start with something small, manageable, and meaningful and see where it takes you!

Reflection

- *If your goal is supporting student learning:* What curricular opportunities do your students have to communicate their ideas, knowledge, questions, understanding, learning, and opinions? What technology do you have access to that might enable students to communicate in that task in a more ideal way?

- *If your goal is supporting professional learning:* What are your options in terms of providing practical support for teachers using technology in their classrooms? Do you have access to technology coaches at the school, district, or state level? Would a peer-mentoring and support system work? Are there confident technology users on staff who could pilot new tools and support colleagues?

- *If your goal is supporting curriculum development:* Do you have a technology curriculum in place that facilitates, encourages, and enables technology as a tool to enhance student communication? Do your wider curriculum documents reference, embed, or integrate technology as a tool to enable and enhance student communication of knowledge, skills, and understandings?

- *If your goal is supporting systems and structures:* Are the resources and infrastructure that are in place sufficient in quantity, reliable, up-to-date, and supportive of pedagogy? What might next steps be in terms of gathering accurate information about current and near-future pedagogical needs and taking action to meet those needs through systems, structures, and resources?

05

Pedagogy

Enhancing Student Collaboration

The emphasis on collaboration in learning, work, and life has changed a great deal in recent decades. This is partly a result of technological advancement and partly because the prevailing view of what makes a good worker or learner has been changing over time, placing more value on the ability to work and problem solve in collaboration with others than on the ability to work in isolation. Collaborating isn't new: as humans we have always needed to collaborate to survive, but the scope of our collaboration has changed from day-to-day survival to societal advancement and its scale has changed from local to global.

We see it in classrooms, where the traditional rows of individual desks are replaced by group tables, flexible seating, and modular furniture. We see it in higher education, where the world's best universities increasingly demand that students not only master knowledge and skills but also demonstrate the ability to apply their learning to collaborate and work within a team. We see it in the front lines of cutting-edge science, where researchers collaborate with peers around the world to develop new theories, test hypotheses, and share findings.

As the world becomes more connected, collaboration within and between disciplines is changing the way that we tackle the world's biggest problems. Climate change, natural disasters, disease, and humanitarian crises are not single-subject issues—they freely cross the imaginary boundaries between science, social studies, language, and modern history. To tackle them, experts from all disciplines must work together, think conceptually, share knowledge, and ask the questions that their peers in other specialties may not have realized needed to be asked.

These big issues will define future generations. We as educators can play a positive role by preparing our students to work between and across disciplines and to collaborate with others to ask and answer big and complex questions.

Disciplinary or Cross-, Trans-, Multi-, or Interdisciplinary?

In many educational settings the terms *cross-disciplinary, multidisciplinary, transdisciplinary,* and *interdisciplinary* are becoming more common as we strive to provide students with increasingly contextual and meaningful pathways to learning. However, it is not always entirely clear to educators what these terms truly mean and how they should be applied. To an extent, how you define and understand the terms depends a little bit on your education, background, and location as a teacher, as there are international and program-specific variations in how they are applied. While we don't use all of these terms in this chapter, we do reference interdisciplinary and multidisciplinary approaches several times, and we define the various types of discipline as follows (Stember 1991):

- *Disciplinary*: A single-subject approach; teaching the knowledge, skills, and understandings of a given discipline or subject in isolation.

- *Cross-disciplinary*: Considering or viewing one subject or discipline from the perspective of another.

- *Multidisciplinary*: When specialists from different subjects or disciplines draw on their disciplinary knowledge to collaborate.

- *Interdisciplinary*: Synthesizing and integrating knowledge, skills, and understandings from different disciplines together into one approach.

- *Transdisciplinary*: Spanning and overarching the disciplines to emphasize concepts, knowledge, skills, and understandings beyond disciplinary frameworks.

In some of the Illustrating Integration examples we give in this chapter—for example, "Interdisciplinary Migration Study" (page 63) and "Transparent, Trackable Learning" (page 75)—it could be argued that the approach is both multidisciplinary and interdisciplinary, depending on the perspectives of the people involved. For the teachers, who in this example are subject specialists, the approach may be multidisciplinary: they must each utilize their specialist disciplinary knowledge to create a collaborative learning opportunity for their students. The students are then aiming to work in an interdisciplinary way, bringing together and synthesizing the learning from these different disciplines.

Collaborating in the Classroom and Beyond

Today, collaboration is such an embedded expectation in how we learn and work that sometimes we, as educators, can forget how complex and demanding it is to truly and meaningfully collaborate with others. We must determine how to give ourselves the space and permission necessary to explore what collaboration is, ask ourselves why we place importance on it, and think about what we need to do to teach it effectively.

The generally agreed upon definition of collaboration as "working together toward a shared goal" sounds simple and straightforward, but in reality, high-quality collaboration is very difficult to achieve. This is partly because we tend to think of collaboration as being a skill in and of itself, when it is actually a process in which we apply a collection of other related skills (such as listening, negotiating, communicating, compromising, organizing, prioritizing, and self-management) in context. We found that when we asked ourselves the following questions about collaboration, they were often very difficult to answer:

- Why do we tend to value collaboration in the classroom as much as, or sometimes more than, individual learning?

- What learning purposes is collaboration most suited to supporting?

- How and why do we as educators make the decision to choose a collaborative approach over an individual approach? Do we make that decision consciously and, if so, on what grounds?

- What, if anything, is the difference between group work and collaboration?

- What skills are necessary for our students to develop in order to be effective collaborators? How and when do we teach those skills?

- What does authentic and effective collaboration really look like, both within and beyond the classroom?

In trying to answer these questions for ourselves, we turned to a wide range of research and the experiences of professionals around the world. We found that for many teachers, ourselves included, the presumed benefits of collaboration are taken so much for granted that few teachers are actually trained in what collaboration really is, why it matters, and, most importantly, how to support or structure it effectively.

We believe that technology's potential in the context of collaboration goes far beyond the potential for global collaboration that is most commonly thought of as the end goal. Certainly, collaborating with strangers or peers around the world on a project or problem is a valuable application of technology, but we can and should be leveraging technology in sustainable and everyday ways to help our students build the transferrable skills they need to be effective collaborators within their own schools and classrooms and to overcome many of the traditional classroom barriers to everyday collaboration.

In this chapter we explore how you can make use of technology to facilitate and enhance collaboration in your classroom or context. To do this, we frame student collaboration around what we see as being three key purposes for student collaboration:

- forming understanding

- building community

- managing tasks and sharing information

In each of these sections we present practical examples for technology-enhanced application of collaboration in three general categories, which range in scope from in-class partners to working with peers and experts around the world:

- *Within group*: This type of collaboration includes partners, small groups, or even whole classes working together on a task or learning experience within the same homeroom or subject, with a single teacher. Most of the daily collaboration that takes place in classrooms is likely to be at the within-group level.

- *Between groups*: This might involve students of the same age or grade collaborating between different classes, students of the same age or grade collaborating between different subjects, or students of different ages or grades collaborating on the same or different subjects. Collaboration of this type offers exciting, innovative opportunities for students to work beyond single-subject, disciplinary boundaries and to learn from students who have different needs and strengths.

- *Beyond school*: When we help our students to reach out beyond the boundaries of their school to connect with peers from different cultures and contexts, this can create rich and meaningful learning experiences. Similarly, working with experts from around the world can help students to add layers of deeper meaning and real-world context to otherwise classroom-based learning.

The examples and approaches we share are based on the core academic subjects of language arts, math, social studies, and science. They are designed to be transferable to different age groups and subjects across the curriculum to inspire you to explore how technology could enhance collaboration in your school and classroom, whatever age or subject you specialize in.

Forming Understanding

Most teachers accept that the process of learning is co-constructive (think back to your teacher training about Vygotsky and constructivism); in essence, students learn from each other at least as much as they learn from us. By working with peers who are stronger in some areas and weaker in others, students have a variety of opportunities, such as

- learning by explaining as well as being explained to,

- being confronted with questions they may never have thought to ask, and

- having the chance to ask questions they might feel unwilling to ask their teacher.

Integrating technology into how we support the formation of understanding in the classroom allows us to streamline and enhance this process, making it more accessible and more manageable.

Digital collaboration can offer a platform for students to work individually or in small groups to collect, analyze, and synthesize learning as part of a larger goal. For example, in science students might explore a shared hypothesis through a range of experiments, collecting their results in a shared collaborative digital space in order to form understanding and draw conclusions. In any subject students might use a collaborative digital space to ask questions throughout a unit or topic—commenting on, answering, or extending questions as their learning progresses.

These approaches are also ideal for supporting differentiation through low-threshold, high-ceiling (LTHC) learning engagements (Papert 1980), in which all students can participate in a shared learning task but work at different levels depending on their ability and engagement. Through digital collaboration platforms, students can gain a window into the possibilities of the task, gaining and giving support through the struggles and successes of their peers.

Within-Group Collaboration

The use of mind maps to support students in creating connections between their own individual ideas, skills, concepts, and knowledge is well established in many classrooms. Mind maps allow students to make and see connections between different thoughts and ideas and are usually done at an individual level, on paper. There is, of course, much benefit for students in making these connections at the personal level, but by adding in a collaborative digital mind-mapping tool, such as through Popplet or Padlet, we can take that a step further, moving beyond the individual level so that students can work co-constructively at a whole-class or group level. With this approach they can make even deeper and richer connections between current and prior learning, building on and contributing to the understanding of others as well as themselves. Collaborating in this way can also be a valuable way of building the interpersonal and self-management skills students will need to employ in digital collaborative experiences throughout school and beyond, as they gain experience in respecting the input of others, building on their understanding in new ways, and collaborating over a longer period of time, rather than only in short group-work bursts.

Illustrating Integration: Mind Maps in Math

In math, students are learning about how to find the length of an unknown side of a triangle using the quadratic equation. In order to understand and apply the quadratic equation, students need to draw on and apply their prior knowledge and conceptual understanding of geometry, algebra, order of operations, integers, variables, fractions, and more. To support the students in this, their teacher introduces a collaborative digital mind-mapping tool, which the students contribute to over the course of their learning. With the help of some initial teacher modeling and support—as well as ongoing guidance and facilitation—the students slowly add and refer to this mind map. With it they record questions, understandings, and connections between different areas as their understanding of how the different math skills and concepts they have learned so far relate to the quadratic equation, and its practical application expands. This visual and concrete record of learning acts as a support for students who are struggling, as well as providing an opportunity for extension for students who can use it to make advanced conceptual connections and explore questions posed by peers.

Mind mapping can support within-group formation of understanding in numerous other ways, for example:

- *Math*: making connections between addition, repeated addition, and multiplication; subtraction, division, fractions, and decimals; and area, multiplication, and squaring

- *Social studies*: creating a richer, shared understanding of the complex and interconnected factors surrounding a historical or modern war, human migration, or other current topic

- *Language*: exploring class or group novels, grammar structures, spelling conventions, and word origins and meanings

Between-Group Collaboration

The major issues and opportunities humanity faces, now and in the future, are multidisciplinary ones. Any complex human concern you can think of, from humanitarian crises, to politics, to technological development, to health, will not be solved by environmental scientists, policy makers, or health specialists working in isolation. Addressing issues like these will require experts from multiple disciplines to work together. As educators we have a critical role to play in that process by teaching our students how to make connections between disciplines and find solutions to complex problems, but to do this we have to learn to teach in a more dynamic way.

In middle and high school in particular, it can be challenging to create the structures and systems necessary to facilitate connections between different subjects, even though science and math complement each other in fundamental ways, as do social studies, literature, and the arts. The current system of discrete subjects makes sense when we are constrained by space and time to the degree that we are in the traditional schooling system. However, technology can enable collaboration in a way that transcends those barriers, and we can use it to enhance and support collaboration between groups in ways that open up exciting opportunities to build and sustain interdisciplinary links.

Illustrating Integration:
Interdisciplinary Migration Study

Grade 8 students have been hearing a lot about immigration on the news and asking questions in their classes. To reflect and build on this interest, their English, history, geography, and art and design teachers have agreed to collaborate, planning a multi- or interdisciplinary unit of study around the theme of human migration.

In English, the students read a selection of novels about the experiences of young people who emigrate from their home countries for a variety of reasons, analyzing features of the texts, making inferences, and summarizing for their classmates. In history, the students explore the history of immigration to the United States, by investigating primary sources like texts and photographs, considering the impacts of immigration on US culture, and identifying different perspectives related to historical immigration. In geography, the students learn about the geographical features and climates of countries they have heard about in the news in relation to human migration. They study different types of maps and explore links between conflict, natural resources, and climate. In art and design, the students explore and reflect on works of art created by people who have immigrated to the United States or which were inspired by forces that often drive emigration, such as war, food shortage, climate change, and unemployment.

To support the students in making connections between these disciplines, and to enable the teachers to keep track of what the students are learning and understanding in other classes, they use a collaborative digital platform, such as Google Classroom, Moodle, or Edmodo, which enables teachers and students to create a shared space where the logistics of working in an interdisciplinary way are simplified and the experience is enhanced (more on the specifics of this in "Illustrating Integration: Transparent, Trackable Learning" on page 75).

By actively and deliberately making connections between and across subjects, the students have the opportunity to explore human migration through various disciplines and consider many different perspectives, causes, and impacts. Not only does this give them a deeper, more transferable understanding of the causes and effects of human migration at the global and human levels, but it helps to reinforce the experience of learning in an interdisciplinary way. Rather than learning about geography in one disciplinary classroom and English in another, students experience learning about human migration in an interdisciplinary space.

Applying learning from each discipline in context enables the formation of deeper understanding and meaningful application for the students. In elementary school this approach is already quite common and is much easier to manage since a single teacher usually teaches the majority of the core subjects.

In middle and high school it becomes much more challenging to make and maintain those interdisciplinary connections. It takes time to plan face-to-face meetings with teachers from other subjects, and scheduling often makes this difficult. This approach also requires that those teachers be aware of what is happening in the other subjects in order to ask questions and respond to student interest, developing understandings, and misconceptions.

The power of technology in this context is in how technology can facilitate and support interdisciplinary learning by breaking down logistical barriers that can make collaboration of this type so challenging through traditional teaching methods. Using a digital platform allows students to communicate their questions, knowledge, and developing understandings between different subjects. It provides easy, real-time access for several different teachers to a constantly expanding record of learning. This tangible record helps teachers to keep informed about what is being learned in different subjects, so they can refer to and build upon that learning in their own classroom. And it allows students to refer back to and build on prior learning to deepen their understanding of the overarching interdisciplinary topic as well as the individual disciplines. Whatever age students are, they benefit from the opportunity to make these deep, conceptual connections and relate their learning to real-world contexts.

Forming Understanding: Challenges and Solutions

CHALLENGES	SOLUTIONS
→ Logistics of time and physical space can make bridging separate subjects to develop interdisciplinary understanding of complex situations or concepts difficult. → Students need support and opportunities to build on ongoing learning of themselves and others to find connections between ideas and deepen understanding.	→ Digital classrooms provide a shared, interdisciplinary learning space to which teachers of multiple disciplines contribute. Teachers can easily share digital assignments and resources with students, and students can record and easily refer back to questions and ongoing learning. → Collaborative mind maps allow students within and between groups to share their learning, learn from each other, and see overarching connections between ideas.

To access the regularly updated online resources with more detailed challenges and solutions plus digital approaches and tools, either scan the QR code on page ix or visit Hein.pub/Tech-Resources.

Beyond-School Collaboration

When we extend the concept of collaborative technology beyond the school community, students are able to access an even wider range of knowledge, perspectives, and questions and to form an even richer and more contextual level of understanding in their learning. Students who are separated by geography, but who are exploring similar topics, can connect through digital learning journals, blogs, or class websites to view, reflect, and comment on each other's learning.

For students who would benefit from additional support or who are learning above their grade level, technology can provide a way of collaborating with others beyond their classroom. In "Illustrating Integration: Mind Mapping in Math" we gave an example of using collaborative mind maps to help students make connections between different math concepts and skills within their group. We can use the same approach to, for example, provide an opportunity for a student who is working above their grade level or beyond the curriculum to connect with students in other schools who have the same needs and strengths.

Similarly, we can extend the scope of the example given in "Illustrating Integration: Interdisciplinary Migration Study" and consider ways in which we could use technology to help students to collaborate with peers or experts outside their own school community.

Illustrating Integration: Collaborative Bulletin Board for Body Unit

Mrs. Shaughnessy's fifth-grade class is learning about the human body, how its systems interconnect, and how they are interdependent. They are students at an international school in a primarily non-English-speaking host country, yet many of the students do not speak the host country's main language. This means that bringing an expert into the classroom presents challenges for many of the students, as does finding a local expert who is confident in answering complex questions about human biology in English. To support them with their research into the human body, Mrs. Shaughnessy has arranged a collaboration with a medical professional, Mr. Symonds, in a different country. As the students research and learn, they gather questions they are not able to answer for themselves on a board in the classroom. Each week, the class discusses and chooses three top questions to ask their expert through Padlet, a collaborative bulletin board. Mr. Symonds knows that the students are learning about how body systems interconnect, so over the course of the week he posts photos, videos, and pictures to help answer the questions and support this larger concept. As the students continue to learn over the weeks, their understanding grows, and they are able to build on the expert's knowledge to form a deeper understanding of the content and the concept behind the topic.

To see the Padlet, visit this link: https://padlet.com/mrs_gilmore/ body_unit

Today, students and teachers can take advantage of a huge range of digital tools to facilitate collaboration with experts around the world who can support and motivate student learning, such as in the vignette on the human body unit. Video-calling software can connect classes with experts in real time, while collaborative bulletin boards can allow experts and students to leave each other video, audio, images, or text to which users can respond at convenient times.

We can use the same technology to connect students with peers in communities beyond their schools to discuss and inquire into any number of different concepts. Facilitating contact between students from different cultures, contexts, and communities can provoke, inspire, and support a deeper and richer level of inquiry, while giving students the chance to ask questions of each other, clarify, and make deeper connections between the content and real-world aspects of the otherwise academic topics they are studying.

Building Community

Every class comprises many individuals with varying strengths, needs, backgrounds, and daily experiences. For teachers and students alike, learning about those differences, finding common ground, and developing empathy and mutual understanding are key to building a functional and respectful learning community.

Within-Group Collaboration

Word-cloud tools, such as Poll Everywhere or Mentimeter, can help teachers and students to find out how the members of their class are feeling by offering a creative and informal way of allowing students to share their morning routines, their social experiences at break times, or their feelings during lessons. A collaborative class agenda, for example, through Google Docs, Padlet, or Flipgrid, can provide students with a voice in suggesting the discussion topics for weekly meetings, creating a sense of ownership and responsibility in their class or group community.

Additionally, several digital tools, such as Socrative or Verso App, are designed to allow students to share responses with the teacher while keeping their identity anonymous from each other. Tools like these can be very valuable in enabling students to ask questions and raise concerns they would not normally feel comfortable discussing face-to-face, or in front of their peers, such as concerns around bullying or social issues, health and well-being, or the home.

Illustrating Integration: Daily Poll

Each morning, Mrs. Okoye's students arrive in her classroom, and she wonders how they are feeling. Did they eat breakfast? Did they have a calm or a stressful morning? Is anything concerning them about the day ahead? Has anything exciting happened that should be celebrated? She has tried asking them, but not all students are willing to share details of their lives out loud, and having them write on slips of paper is logistically challenging. To help her gather the information she wants, she turns to polling software. This allows her to pose a question to the class that they can quickly answer, either anonymously or not, depending on the teacher's settings, on school or personal devices. Mrs. Okoye establishes a routine where she posts her question on the board each morning for the students to answer as they arrive, and she can then quickly scan through the responses and follow up with students who she thinks would benefit from support or encouragement, so that they are in the best possible frame of mind to learn.

The approach in the daily poll vignette is relevant for students of every age: as teachers we have no way of knowing what challenges, stresses, or triumphs our students may have faced before they even set foot in our classrooms. Whether they are experiencing conflict at home or with a classmate, skipped breakfast, or slept badly, for example, will have an impact on their ability to concentrate, work with their peers, and be successful in school. With that information, we can be sensitive to their needs and provide support.

Polling software can also be valuable in enabling a way for all students to participate in the class in a less visible way. Not every student feels comfortable raising their hand or being called upon to give an answer. Polling software can allow various degrees of anonymous participation, from making responses truly anonymous (not even the teacher knows who has said what), to hiding the names of participants from other students but allowing the teacher to see them, to displaying the names of participants to each other. This kind of control can be helpful depending on the topic. For example, true anonymity might be desired to encourage students to ask questions or raise concerns during lessons on sex or health education, while the accountability of having names visible to either the teacher or the students can be useful when using the responses to prompt class discussions or respond to each other's questions on a given topic.

Between-Group Collaboration

Students of all ages and abilities have much to gain from working with other students who have different needs, strengths, and areas of expertise. Within a school, the practicalities of arranging collaboration between groups—for example, when it comes to time, schedules, and space—can sometimes create insurmountable challenges.

Illustrating Integration: Digital Reading Classrooms

For many years there has been a reading buddy program between students in different grades. First-grade students read with fourth graders, second grade is buddied with fifth grade, and third grade reads with sixth grade. The program helps children develop relationships across grade levels, increases empathy, and decreases conflict on the playground. It also provides opportunities for EAL (English as an additional language) students to communicate in their mother tongue as well as develop their English skills, while giving confidence to reluctant readers of all ages. Every year the teachers and students start out with high expectations of the reading buddy program, and it usually continues steadily for a few months, but then the demands of the school schedule begin to get in the way. To keep the reading buddy program going, the school sets up digital reading classrooms: the students record themselves reading to their buddies, and later their buddies respond with feedback and reading of their own. The younger students love hearing the older students reading stories to them, and they learn to ask questions and comment on the stories they hear. The older students support the younger students by giving feedback on their fluency and expression and asking questions to prompt text comprehension. Teachers scaffold the process so that the students know how long to read for, what type of feedback to give, and what kinds of questions to ask each other. Because the reading is recorded, the classes can listen, read, and respond whenever their schedule will allow, meaning that when classes can't meet face-to-face, the reading buddy program keeps going strong.

Another way in which we sometimes ask students of different ages and stages to collaborate is in class-mixing or ability-based groups. Technology can be useful in providing us with tools and methods we can use to build groups in ways that are purposeful, while being sensitive to the development of the whole child by expanding our within-group scenario of using digital collaboration to facilitate low-threshold, high-ceiling activities across multiple groups and classes. We can also use technology to create mentoring or mutual support links between students in different grades, which they can use to build common understanding and make connections between their learning when the concepts and skills being covered in class align. In this way we can use technology-supported differentiation and groupings to build competence and understanding while valuing individuals' confidence and self-esteem.

Beyond-School Collaboration

Giving our students the opportunity to learn with and from peers with different life and educational experiences helps to develop empathy, perspective, and social skills. Video-calling technology, online messaging, and internationally accessible collaborative platforms such as Padlet have made it increasingly easy and safe to make connections between students from different sides of the world. However, we don't need to go that far to create opportunities for our students to build community: within a country, or even a single city, students in different schools experience vastly different life and educational experiences. Many of these students may never meet in their daily lives because of geographical, social, or economical barriers.

When connecting with other schools, it is important to remember that varying levels of access to student technology do not need to be a barrier to building community links. Using a single class PC with a connection to the Internet, a cheap microphone, and a webcam, students can record videos to email or share with another class through a website or shared digital learning journal, or they can video-call in real time. With even one Internet-connected device in each school, students from different schools can contribute to a shared digital bulletin board where they ask and answer questions and share their experiences.

Illustrating Integration: Multiclass Habitat Research

Mr. Gillies' grade 4 students were learning about habitats. Mr. Gillies had teacher friends in various countries around the world and also reached out to his PLN on Twitter to ask if there were other classes learning about the same topic who would be interested in connecting. He identified three other classes from different parts of the world who were happy to collaborate. The teachers decided in advance what their students would research about the habitat closest to where they lived (e.g., wildlife, human population, climate, weather, geographical features, common plants) and agreed on a way of sharing that information. To get to know each other, the three classes took turns video chatting with each other, time zones and technology permitting, and saw firsthand the students they were working with as well as the environment outside the classroom. When this was impossible, classes exchanged photos or videos via email or using a shared blog. They then researched their own habitats and used what they learned to create a simple, free website for the other classes to learn from. As they learned about each other's habitats, students gathered questions that they asked using video calls, email, digital bulletin boards, blogs, or any other suitable and accessible platform. At the end of the unit, all three classes had learned about not only their own closest natural habitat but two others around the world from firsthand sources, while making connections with real students beyond their own community.

By connecting students who are working on developing the same skills and learning similar content knowledge, we can give them access to unparalleled primary sources of information and give them an opportunity to inquire in different ways. This can be very useful for topics such as the following:

- geographical features
- water conservation and scarcity
- habitats and wildlife
- population studies
- rural and urban communities
- human migration
- modern foreign languages
- world music and the arts.

For schools where it is an option for students to use social media, or where teachers can use social media on behalf of their students, this can provide limitless opportunities for students to connect with each other and learn from each other by creating their own professional learning networks. Twitter, for example, has for many years offered teachers a way of connecting with other professionals to challenge their own thinking and benefit from shared ideas and resources. The use of hashtags (e.g., #grade8math or #climat-echange) allows users to collect and search for tweets on a given topic, and, with proper training and oversight to ensure that students are behaving responsibly and are making safe connections online, students can also benefit from these networks.

Even more importantly, this approach can build empathy and familiarity with other students whom they might otherwise never get to know. We don't always have to reach around the world: schools mere miles apart may experience completely different learning and living conditions, depending on socioeconomic factors. With collaborative planning and sensitive guidance at the teacher level, technology can provide a way for students from different communities to explore big questions and seek solutions together to provocative and important issues such as privilege, wealth, and equality.

Building Community: Challenges and Solutions

CHALLENGES	SOLUTIONS
→ It is difficult to manage the space and scheduling logistics of working with others in different subjects, grade levels, or ability levels.	→ Video and audio recordings, video calling, and shared digital platforms allow for asynchronous collaboration.
→ It's not easy to provide varied opportunities for students to contribute to class discussions and agendas, ask questions, and raise concerns.	→ Polling tools allow for anonymous or private sharing of questions, answers, feedback, and more.
	→ Teachers can use collaborative word clouds to create a snapshot of group or class concerns, needs, questions, or moods.
	→ Digital bulletin boards can save space and provide easy access for students to share questions, post topics for class meetings, and so on.

To access the regularly updated online resources with more detailed challenges and solutions plus digital approaches and tools, either scan the QR code on page ix or visit Hein.pub/Tech-Resources.

Managing Tasks and Sharing Information

Logistics pose some of the most challenging day-to-day aspects of student collaboration. How can we keep track of which students are responsible for which elements of a collaborative task? How can students keep track of their own responsibilities and deadlines and those of their peers? How can everyone involved access and track the group's work in a way that is manageable and efficient?

The nature of a truly collaborative task requires students to be able to access, reflect upon, give feedback on, and plan based on each other's work in a timely, ongoing way. Digital platforms like collaborative digital classrooms (e.g., Google Classroom), digital bulletin boards (e.g., Padlet), or cloud-based word-processing platforms (e.g., Google Drive) are particularly suited to facilitating and supporting these precise needs in a way that traditional, paper-based methods are not. They do this by allowing multiple individuals to access and work on shared multimedia projects and documents simultaneously or not, from anywhere in the world, while paper-based methods require learners to take turns accessing and borrowing documents, necessitating a very individual approach to something intended to be collaborative.

Within-Group Collaboration

Using technology for within-group collaboration can be very rewarding as it will enable you and your students to enhance and streamline methods of collaboration in a particularly visible way that will be noticed in the day-to-day workings of the class. Spotting opportunities to enhance collaboration within a group is very simple: look for tasks, subjects, or learning engagements where you expect your students to work in groups, and consider what aspects of those group-work situations feel inauthentic, difficult to manage, or less than ideal for you or for your students. You can remedy those issues through technology, which can make the process of learning more transparent for your students and for you and remove barriers to sharing materials and communicating progress and ideas. The following examples may help you to identify some of these barriers and opportunities within your own classroom.

Illustrating Integration: Collaborative Bulletin Boards for Literature Circles

In language arts, students are expected to work in a group to read, discuss, analyze, and respond to a novel. To facilitate this, the class' teacher, Mrs. Strand, has set up literature circle groups in which each member has designated roles and responsibilities. Traditionally these groups have worked in individual paper notebooks. Mrs. Strand feels that the literature circles have the potential to be an excellent strategy for encouraging deep exploration and comprehension of texts, but they are difficult to track and manage. It is difficult for other members to refer to and build on the work each group member creates in a paper notebook, and it is time-consuming for Mrs. Strand to access and respond to each notebook. It can be difficult for students to track who has read up to which page, whose turn it is to take on which role in the group, how each student can access others' work, and how they can efficiently share their learning with Mrs. Strand for feedback.

To alleviate these issues, Mrs. Strand creates simple collaborative bulletin boards for each group using Padlet. Mrs. Strand chooses this type of platform for its ease of use and simplicity of access (individual accounts are not needed for students, and Padlets can be accessed by link or QR code) and for the potential to add content in a variety of formats including audio, drawings, photos, videos, and text. Using this platform, groups log their reflections and work on their shared bulletin board from home or class, share their learning and developing understanding in creative and flexible ways, and link to more extensive digital written tasks stored in other digital platforms (e.g., in Google Drive). Rather than searching through and cross-referencing multiple notebooks, Mrs. Strand can now easily log in to check progress in one digital place, provide feedback to individuals and the whole group, and take advantage of the different media formats to assess student learning in ways that were previously not possible.

For students working on a shared research or writing task, collaborative digital platforms can be invaluable in providing clarity around shared tasks and responsibilities and project timelines and in facilitating feedback to multiple students on a single project.

For the teacher, they provide a window into current progress, future stumbling blocks, and the group dynamic as well as creating a permanent physical record of the process of collaboration to use as a basis for reflection, assessment, and future planning.

Between-Group Collaboration

As hard as it is for one teacher to keep track of students collaborating within a single group when that involves collecting and comparing multiple paper notebooks or conferencing regularly with individual students, that task becomes exponentially more difficult for two or more teachers, often working in conflicting schedules, with their individual pressures and priorities. One of technology's great strengths in this model of collaboration is in creating channels of communication and a record of process, progress, and accountability for both teachers and students.

The approaches used to manage tasks and share information when groups collaborate on the within-group level become increasingly valuable when collaboration is scaled up to the between-group level.

Shared task lists, project calendars with due dates and explicit information about the stages of the project or collaboration, and mutually accessible resources such as research guides, assignments, and supportive teaching materials such as videos can be easily shared and tracked to enable transparency and accountability throughout the process. Most digital classroom platforms support multiple teachers per "class," meaning that teachers from different subjects or physical classes can easily access the same digital class at whatever time and in whatever location is most convenient.

Illustrating Integration: Transparent, Trackable Learning

In *"Illustrating Integration: Interdisciplinary Migration Study"* (page 63), we described the experiences of a group of eighth-grade students who engaged in a unit of study on human migration, using a collaborative digital platform, such as Google Classroom, Moodle, or Edmodo.

The students benefited from learning about this complex issue in an interdisciplinary way by developing a deeper understanding of the global factors that contribute to migration as well as human perspectives around migration from several standpoints. Using a digital platform to facilitate this approach further benefited the students and teachers by making the process of learning transparent, trackable, and manageable across several different classes, in a way that would not have been possible using paper-based methods.

Rather than separate teachers monitoring separate notebooks and finding a way to update colleagues on students' progress, all teachers could see the digital assignments in one centralized location. This transparency and ease of access facilitated collaboration between the teachers, who could see, build on, and refer to assignments from other subjects. In addition to assignments, teachers could easily share digital resources such as videos, images, and websites for students and collaborating teachers to refer to. For the students, having all their assignments, learning journals, and resources centralized in one place made sense logistically as well as conceptually. Working in a digital, collaborative platform, students can easily pose questions to teachers and other collaborators and refer back to answers because they are stored digitally; collaborate remotely on assignments; and refer to resources and learning from different subjects with ease.

Beyond-School Collaboration

Today's students are busier than they have ever been, but the ability to collaborate not in real time means that scheduling conflicts are much less of a barrier to collaboration. With video-, audio-, or text-based messaging, students can ask and answer questions when time permits, even if location doesn't. Video conferencing can easily enable large groups of students to meet virtually. These approaches are increasingly becoming the norm in higher education as larger cohorts of students and distance-learning opportunities drive the need for virtual learning environments.

Illustrating Integration:
Jenny

Jenny is an extremely able student who is, in some subjects, working beyond the level that her school can accommodate. To provide Jenny with the academic challenge she needs, as well as the courses she needs to be able to follow her chosen path when she gets to college, her school seeks out other schools who are using digital classroom platforms, such as Google Classroom or Moodle, and who offer the advanced classes Jenny needs. Jenny virtually joins these classes, submitting her assignments digitally and video conferencing with teachers and students from these other schools when she needs to for more input and discussion.

Access to different or advanced courses, such as in Jenny's case, is one application for beyond-school digital collaboration of this type, but this might also benefit students who are, for example,

- injured or unwell and cannot physically attend school;

- homeschooled and would benefit from some involvement in formal classes;

- in need of specialist learning support that is not available in their physical location; or

- wishing to supplement or extend their education by learning in an additional language.

Managing Tasks and Sharing Information: Challenges and Solutions

CHALLENGES	SOLUTIONS
➤ It is hard to track the status of shared tasks.	➤ Digital classrooms and bulletin boards provide group access to a shared work space.
➤ It is time-consuming for group members and teachers to access individuals' work.	➤ Task lists, project timelines, and outstanding tasks are visible to all group members and synchronized.
➤ Teachers often struggle to ensure individual accountability and make responsibility visible.	

To access the regularly updated online resources with more detailed challenges and solutions plus digital approaches, either scan the QR code on page ix or visit Hein.pub/Tech-Resources.

As going to college or a university continues to become more common for students, distance learning and virtual learning environments are becoming increasingly common in order to meet demand and facilitate the learning of larger and larger groups. Experiencing learning in this way earlier in their school careers may help students to develop valuable skills and understandings they will draw upon if they encounter this type of learning beyond school.

Next Steps

Consider where the barriers against collaboration lie for yourself and your students: where do time, space, or logistics prevent you from achieving your ideal vision for a collaborative activity or process?

By situating collaboration within the broad purposes of managing shared tasks, building community, and forming understanding, you can be clear about what you want your students to achieve through collaborating. From there you can identify what level of collaboration (within group, between groups, or beyond school) might be most effective in helping your students achieve that goal.

Reflection

- *If your goal is supporting student learning:* What skills and understandings do you explicitly teach to support your students' ability to collaborate effectively? How might collaboration between groups or beyond school support or enhance the learning of your students?

- *If your goal is supporting professional learning:* What opportunities exist for staff members to experience and explicitly practice collaboration in their own professional learning? Are digital platforms used at the staff level to support teacher inquiry and professional development?

- *If your goal is supporting curriculum development:* Does the curriculum articulate and support the development of collaborative skills and understandings?

- *If your goal is supporting systems and structures:* Are opportunities available for teachers to learn about and explore digital platforms that support collaboration?

Pedagogy

Planning, Scaffolding, and Integrating Technology

After reading Chapters 4 and 5, we hope you have gained a deeper understanding of the purposes underlying meaningful technology integration, or the *why* of technology integration. At this point, though, you may be wondering how to put these ideas into practice. Perhaps you are completely new to integrating technology, or you have had tried to integrate technology and found that the student process or outcome has not always matched your hopes or plans. An understanding of how to plan for and scaffold technology integration in the classroom will help you and the teachers in your context to teach with and through technology effectively, successfully, and sustainably.

In this chapter we will guide you through the process of reframing the way you integrate technology in your classroom, by putting the core learning objective at the center of planning, identifying whether and how technology can enhance learning engagements, and applying your knowledge and skill to scaffold and support student learning with technology.

We know that the last thing any teacher needs is another add-on, but when technology is integrated effectively it is not an add-on; it is a tool that can enhance how you teach and how your students learn. Throughout this chapter we aim to guide you to identify when technology integration makes sense and enhances learning, not so that you can do *more*, but so you can do what you do optimally. Planning for and integrating technology takes mindful consideration, but like most things it will soon become a natural part of your thinking process.

First Steps First: Starting from Where You Are

Before we dive into the nuts and bolts of planning for and implementing technology within classroom lessons, take a moment to reflect on your current practice and mindset. This process will help you calibrate and identify where your current practice lives on the spectrum of technology integration.

Take a moment to read the teacher descriptions that follow. Do you identify with one, more than one, or aspects of all of the descriptions? What are the cornerstones of your beliefs regarding technology integration, and how have they impacted the level and frequency with which you meaningfully integrate technology within the classroom?

Teacher One is an established teacher within the profession and the school. The teacher has strong beliefs about the role of the teacher and students within the classroom. They are apprehensive about using technology beyond what is required in order to communicate and function within the school on a day-to-day basis. However, the teacher attentively attends technology support sessions and willingly tries new applications and tools within this supportive setting. They welcome other professionals to work with students to integrate technology within the classroom but don't make it a priority in their personal planning and classroom practice.

Teacher Two strongly believes in improving classroom practices through professional learning opportunities and is eager to try new methods and technologies within the classroom. The teacher is easily overwhelmed at times by the amount and variety of technologies that are available within the profession. At times this leads to a disconnect between tool selection and purpose. They spend most of their planning time considering the implementation of the technology rather than the purpose and level of effectiveness. The teacher quickly references professional learning texts but forgets to reference curriculum when planning for learning.

Teacher Three is an avid technology user in their personal life and actively consumes information regarding technology use within the classroom. While the teacher is able to troubleshoot technology problems and eager to integrate technology within the daily routines of the classroom, they have trouble planning in a way that supports both student learning related to content understanding, and technology skills and understanding. At times, the teacher overestimates the students' abilities to effectively use technology and make suitable technological choices related to the purpose of the task.

Teacher Four uses technology in their personal life and values the meaningful use of technology in the classroom. The teacher openly discusses their thoughts and ideas and seeks support when they are unsure of how to use a tool or application within the classroom. They take an active role of meaningfully planning for technology integration including thinking through both the content understanding and the technology skills and understandings. The teacher can effectively scaffold learning within a lesson to ensure that students can connect their learning and proceed through the lesson with the needed technology skills and understandings. They are willing to take risks and are honestly reflective when evaluating the effectiveness of technology integration.

We believe that meaningful and embedded technology integration creates richer and more connected learning experiences for students, but we do not believe that there is only one description of what that can look like. Looking at the descriptions above, you may recognize elements of your practice in one, some, or each of them. Whether previously technology integration has been an add-on, embedded, or somewhere in between in your classroom, you have valuable experiences and a worthwhile foundation upon which you can build.

Every teacher is beginning or continuing this journey from a different position and moving at a different pace. We are not asking you to integrate technology today, tomorrow, or even in a week. Meaningful technology integration doesn't happen overnight, and it is never finished: you will always be learning and adapting your practice as technology changes and your professional understanding of pedagogy continues to develop. As you read on, identify elements of practice that you already have in place, notice ideas that might develop your practice further, and begin to look for opportunities where technology integration would enhance student learning. Then you can begin looking forward and planning for integration, one step at a time.

Strategies for Technology Integration

Technology integration looks different in different classrooms and at different times in the same classroom. When we integrate technology in teaching and learning, we typically do so by using one of three different strategies: *the self-contained lesson*, *embedded integration*, and *multilesson projects*. Not all technology integration fits neatly into these categories, and you may find yourself blending strategies or even creating your own, but we focus on these three to provide a shared vocabulary and foundation for planning and discussion.

Self-Contained Lessons

In a self-contained lesson, technology is integrated into a single lesson to support student learning. The technology used will be connected to the core learning objectives of that lesson but will most likely not bridge beyond that lesson. For example, students might have the learning objective to use different types of questions and use video-calling software, such as Skype or FaceTime, to communicate with an expert beyond school. Or, students might be exploring a learning objective related to angles by coding robots to draw a given polyhedron. This approach may be about enhancing the *process* of learning, for example, through video calling or coding, or it may involve the creation of a digital *product* of some kind, such as an illustration.

Embedded Integration

Embedded integration is when technology is embedded into daily classroom routines or student learning experiences in an ongoing, day-to-day capacity. This could be the use of a digital learning journal or portfolio for students and the teacher to use throughout the day. It might involve the regular use of collaborative platforms (see Chapter 5) to enable students to gather ideas and work together on novel studies, differentiated math content, or other everyday learning engagements. With embedded integration, the focus is most heavily on enhancing the process of day-to-day learning in the classroom and will probably not result in a final digital product to share.

Multilesson Projects

Multilesson projects are defined by teachers and students engaging in multiple, connected lessons where technology integration and content knowledge are scaffolded over time to support an end product. Students might work together to plan and create a product, such as a web page, movie, or podcast, or they might engage in a larger-scale collaborative project involving a whole class or grade level, such as in a performance or an exhibition. Multilesson projects usually end with a final product of some kind, often connected to assessed outcomes.

It is important to note that these strategies are not hierarchical: self-contained lesson integration is not less valuable or challenging than a project, for example. In fact, embedded integration and deliberate, targeted self-contained lesson integration are often the most purposeful integration strategies for our students, as they focus more on enhancing and breaking down barriers during the process of learning and less on creating final products. Each strategy offers different opportunities to enhance student learning, and which strategy you choose should depend on what the purpose of the learning is.

In the next part of this chapter we will guide you through the process of planning for, scaffolding, and realizing technology integration. You can apply that process to all three of these strategies, but as you read, try to refer back and consider which parts of the process might be more or less challenging in different strategies. For example, scaffolding may be less of an issue in a self-contained lesson but more challenging in a larger or longer project.

As you begin the process of planning for integration, depending on your comfort level, you might find the self-contained lesson to be the most natural starting point. As your confidence builds and you put more and more systems in place within the classroom, your ability to recognize the potential for meaningful technology integration through other strategies will also increase.

Preference Versus Purpose

As student learning always drives this work, we encourage you to keep lesson purpose at the forefront of your thinking when planning and implementing technology integration. This will require you to be critically selective when choosing technology that will enhance teaching. At times all teachers, us included, can be prone to choosing technology tools and applications that we are more comfortable with personally. We need to be mindful of making choices about technology that are based on purpose rather than preference and that put the students at the center of our decision-making.

Soon, thinking about and considering technology integration will become a natural part of your planning process.

The Intechgrate Approach

Moving toward planning for and implementing technology integration in your classroom means moving away from technology as an add-on and toward technology as an embedded and purposeful component of learning and teaching. To support teachers in doing this, we have created the Intechgrate Approach to make the process of planning for, scaffolding, and realizing effective technology integration clearer and more articulated. (See Figure 6.1.)

The Intechgrate Approach to Integrating Technology in the Classroom

Figure 6.1

**Integrating Technology
Online Resources**

*To access a downloadable
and printable **Intechgrate
Approach Outline** from the
online resources, either scan
the QR code on page ix or visit
Hein.pub/Tech-Resources*

The six steps outlined in the Intechgrate Approach apply to all levels of integration, all levels of teacher competency, and all levels of resources. As you read this chapter you may think that it seems like a lot to think about, and in the beginning it can be! But just as everyday teaching strategies and planning have become second nature to you, these steps will become simply a part of how you plan and teach with the tools available to you and your students. Most importantly, by training yourself to think about and plan for technology integration in this way, you will ensure that when you do use technology in your classroom it will benefit your students and support their learning.

Step 1: Identify the Core Learning

The Intechgrate Approach to planning for technology integration begins by asking you to identify the core learning for the lesson. We define core learning as the main learning objectives: What do you actually want your students to learn? What is the real learning objective? This may be content knowledge, conceptual understanding, or the development of essential skills such as social skills, communication skills, collaboration, or self-management. At times when planning, we can get so caught up in the excitement of planning the learning engagement (activity) and the inclusion of technology that our focus is pulled away from the purpose of the lessons.

Just as the Intechgrate Model places student learning at its center, so does the Intechgrate Approach to integrating technology in the classroom. Core learning must remain our focus throughout the planning, implementation, and reflection process; it can be easy to be distracted from it unless we are consciously aware of the need to retain that focus.

Once you have established the core learning, ask this question: Will technology integration enhance the teaching and learning? You may decide at this point that the core learning for the lesson will not be enhanced by the integration of technology or that there isn't a natural opportunity to connect technology to the content, skills, process, or product. Technology isn't always the right fit, and as long as your decision is rooted in purpose and student learning, then we fully support it.

If technology integration will support or enhance student learning, then you need to consider how best to do this.

Step 2: Think Big—Outline the Process

Having identified the core learning and decided that you will plan for technology integration, it's time to think about the big-picture *how* of the teaching. Within this step you'll consider your particular student group to evaluate what strengths and areas of need you'll want to keep in mind.

How will you assess student learning at the conclusion?

How will you know whether the students have learned what you wanted them to learn? How can you assess it? What will students be able to do that they could not do before, or what will they now know or understand? Using the identified core learning as a guide, think carefully about what the intended student learning outcome of the lesson should be. Once you have a clear picture of where you want the students to be at the end of the lesson, consider and identify what assessment will best allow the students to demonstrate that learning. You might recognize this approach as being based on the Understanding by Design (UbD) framework created by Wiggins and McTighe (2011), where teachers begin with curricular outcomes and then plan activities to meet them, rather than the other way around.

What learning engagement will maximize student learning?

At this point you have a beginning (learning objective) and an ending (detailed assessment) for student learning. You now need to fill in the middle by designing the learning engagement (activity) that will most effectively extend their level of knowledge, skill, or understanding to meet the learning objective. At this point in the process, don't try to think specifically about a technology-related engagement. Instead, consider what you would do with your students in an ideal world: what would be the very best learning engagement to meet your purpose, if all barriers were removed and anything were possible? Doing this will help you build toward deciding whether technology integration will allow you to realize that ideal-world learning engagement.

What technology tool will enhance your teaching and student learning?

Begin by considering where within the planned learning engagement technology could replace a tool you currently use, enhance a process, or break down a barrier to get you closer to your ideal-world learning scenario. You could return to the 3 Cs and consider how technology might enhance communication, collaboration, or the construction of understanding. Remember, technology shouldn't be an add-on; it should be an evolution of your practice.

This is also the natural point to consider the technology resources that are available to you and in what quantity. Be flexible in your thinking as far as the logistics within the lesson. Carefully consider what would be best for your students, given the purpose of the lesson and your comfort and skill level with technology.

This is sometimes the point where, if we aren't careful, technology can begin to overpower core learning. In "Illustrating Integration: Persuasive Writing 1," consider the teacher's approach to planning for using iMovie as a tool to support the learning objective to "write arguments to support claims with clear reasons and relevant evidence" (Common Core Standard ELA-LITERACY.W.8.1).

Illustrating Integration: Persuasive Writing 1

To help students meet the core learning objective and persuasive writing skills Mr. Smith has identified, he plans a learning engagement in which students will create political campaign advertisements in iMovie to present an argument for their election to a position of responsibility within the classroom.

Mr. Smith begins by introducing his students to iMovie, allowing them to explore and play with the tool. He supports them to identify where and how to add the photos, videos, and text they will need to create their advertisements. As a class, Mr. Smith and his students look at examples of campaign advertisements for inspiration, and his students then work to create campaign advertisements of their own.

> *Once the advertisements are complete, Mr. Smith is disappointed to find that, while the videos themselves are interesting and technically quite well made, the content has not met the original writing learning objectives. The campaign videos look good, but they aren't particularly clear or persuasive and don't show evidence that the students have learned what he originally set out to teach.*

In the iMovie vignette, Mr. Smith began with a clear learning objective but quickly became distracted from it by the tool. He introduced the tool as the main purpose of the lesson and focused on the product as opposed to the learning process. Compare this with "Illustrating Integration: Persuasive Writing 2."

Illustrating Integration: Persuasive Writing 2

> *Mrs. Becker's students are working toward the same goal as Mr. Smith's using the same tool: iMovie. Just as she would if the students were to be completing a traditional writing assignment, she identifies the skills and understandings central to that learning objective. These might include the ability to identify, introduce, and support a claim; reason logically; provide and cite evidence; and use relevant language features and tone.*
>
> *Mrs. Becker plans and scaffolds the process for her students to do necessary research, create claims, gather ideas and evidence, and develop genre-specific language skills. At the point where previously she might have introduced an essay format for the students to synthesize and communicate their learning, Mrs. Becker instead introduces the format of campaign advertisement.*
>
> *When teaching essay writing as a skill, Mrs. Becker typically leads the students through several steps: she shows them high- and low-quality examples of essays, and they look for features of each; they use or create a rubric to assess their own and past essays; and they learn the desired structure for an essay. In this case, the students go through the same process in learning about the structure and features of high-quality video campaign advertisements.*
>
> *Only after students have gone through this process does Mrs. Becker introduce iMovie. She gives the students time to explore it, supporting*

them to identify where and how to add the photos, videos, and text
they will need to create their advertisements.
    Using the content and language skills they have developed
throughout the learning process, the students create a written plan
and write a script before using iMovie to create a persuasive campaign
advertisement. Once the videos are completed, Mrs. Becker assesses
them against the rubric and finds that the students have met the
stated learning objectives.

For Mrs. Becker, the process of planning for the learning objective is the same, regardless of the tool she is using. She knows that there is a range of knowledge, skills, and understandings that students need to develop, and she plans and scaffolds for those using the same high-quality teaching strategies regardless of whether students are writing an essay or creating an iMovie.

What approach will best meet the needs of your students?

For some students, depending on their developmental stage, it may be appropriate to have time to explore and play with the technology tools prior to the lesson. It may be effective to pull a small cohort of students together prior to the lesson to get a feel for students' level of comfort with a specific technology tool. Consider your students and then decide what would be the most comprehensive way to get a feel for their level of knowledge with regard to the technology. This will not only help facilitate groups but also help you detect what misconceptions may exist and need clarification.

All students come into our classrooms with prior knowledge and experiences that can support or hinder their learning. At this point you will also need to consider the varying levels of learning within the classroom. You, as an education professional, have a strong understanding of the students within your classroom and have probably naturally already begun to think about what aspects of the lesson will need to be scaffolded or differentiated to meet the needs of your students. Think carefully within the context of the lesson, and identify those areas that you will need to adjust to meet the needs of your students. Just as with the lesson content, you'll need to evaluate the students' level of understanding and use of the technology (technology skills) and scaffold aspects of the technology integration. As these thoughts arise, keep notes and carefully consider what would be the best approach to support the teaching and learning.

These considerations may naturally connect to the size of the group working with technology during the lesson. Ask yourself if the technology integration would be best at a whole-class level, a small-group level, a teacher-modeled level, or in some other way.

Technology Teaching Tip

Students often appear to be very confident with a digital tool, even when they have not used it before. Today's technology is designed to be as intuitive and user-friendly as possible, and skills learned while using one tool or platform often transfer very well to other similar tools and platforms. However, it is important to remember that ability to navigate around or use a digital tool is not the same as being able to use that tool effectively for a purpose. Having the skills of knowing where to click, how to add a photo, or how to edit a piece of video does not necessarily mean that the students know how to take or find high-quality photos, determine which photos will be most effective, or edit a video to achieve the purpose you have defined. As the teacher, part of your job when integrating technology will be to look beyond the surface-level skills students have (which may seem to you to be far more advanced than your own!) and teach them how to build on those skills and to how to apply them meaningfully and effectively for the purpose of the core learning.

Step 3: Plan and Scaffold Technology Integration

Once you have a clear idea of which technology you will integrate and how you plan to integrate it, the next step is to revisit your notes and consider what prior knowledge the students have specifically related to technology skills and understandings.

We have often worked with teachers who have used a tool with their students, for example, iMovie, and complained that the final product was not of a high standard. Perhaps the sound was poor, the lighting in the video or photos was too low, the video was too long or too short, or, most importantly, the final video itself did not meet the stated learning objective. When that happens we encourage teachers to look back and reflect on how they scaffolded the learning process for the students and whether it was clear to the students what the features of a high-quality product (in this case, a movie) actually are and how they should demonstrate their understanding of the core learning.

In step 2 we considered the different examples of Mrs. Becker and Mr. Smith in using iMovie to meet a persuasive writing learning objective. In the examples in Figure 6.2, consider how these two different approaches to teaching students to use iMovie itself might yield different final products for Mrs. Becker.

Contrasting Approaches to Planning Integration of iMovie

APPROACH 1	APPROACH 2
Mrs. Becker gave students the task to create a persuasive political campaign advertisement using iMovie.	Mrs. Becker gave students the task to create a persuasive political campaign advertisement using iMovie.
Mrs. Becker clearly communicated the core learning and success criteria related to the language objective of persuasion, and she taught the students the necessary knowledge, skills, and understandings to meet the learning objective.	Mrs. Becker clearly communicated the core learning and success criteria related to the language objective of persuasion, and she taught the students the necessary knowledge, skills, and understandings to meet the learning objective.
Mrs. Becker showed the class examples of professional campaign advertisements for inspiration.	Mrs. Becker showed the class examples of professional campaign advertisements, and the class identified the key features.
Mrs. Becker introduced iMovie as a tool, modeled the different features, and gave the students time to explore and play with the tool before beginning the task.	Mrs. Becker (or, even better, her class) created an assessment rubric for the important features of the campaign advertisement under headings supplied by her, including lighting, sound quality, length, types of shot, on-screen text, and the features of the persuasive writing language objective.
Students worked to gather, record, and create content for their campaign advertisements.	The students planned their campaign advertisements on paper, using the rubric as a guide for quality.

APPROACH 1	APPROACH 2
→ Once the ads were completed, Mrs. Becker assessed the final results.	→ Mrs. Becker introduced iMovie as a tool, modeled the different features, and gave the students time to explore and play with the tool before beginning the task.
	→ (For teachers and students more experienced with using technology to support and enhance learning, this might be the point at which the teacher gives students a guided or free choice about which technology to use. If this is the case, it is important that students are explicit about why they are using the tool they have chosen and how it is most suited to the purpose of the task.)
	→ Students worked to gather, record, and create content for their campaign advertisements, following their plans and referring to their rubric.
	→ Once the ads were completed, Mrs. Becker and her students used the rubric to assess the final result.

Figure 6.2

It's clear that approach 2 will take longer: there are more steps, more planning, and more teacher involvement, but it will be obvious to the students what will be required to be successful in both being persuasive (the core student learning objective) and learning the technology skills needed to create a high-quality product. There may not always be the time available and it might not always be necessary to do each and every one of those steps, but when you are planning for technology integration, consider what your students will need in order to have a meaningful learning experience and plan on that basis. When a tool, learning objective, or approach is very new to you and the students, it is worth taking the time to scaffold effectively.

Once you have identified the technology tool that would best enhance the student learning and you have considered logistics, go back to your lesson plan and review the lesson progression and pacing. If this is the first time your students are using a specific technology tool, there may need to be space within the lesson to support the students' technology skills and understandings. Just as when planning a standard lesson, be mindful of the time it takes to transition and manage tools within the lesson. Does the integration of technology require an element of scaffolding to support the students' ability to find success, and how much time will that take? Will the students require a level of clarity regarding the lesson purpose in order to stay focused on the core learning?

Technology Teaching Tip

It is quite common for teachers go through an initial excitement phase once they begin to integrate technology that leads to the desire to integrate it into every lesson. This can become overwhelming, create technology burnout, and perhaps even distract from core learning over time. While we definitely want to encourage an enthusiastic, open-minded attitude to adopting technology integration, we have not found constant technology use to be the most effective or sustainable way to go. We want to encourage you over time to harness that sense of enthusiasm while becoming selective, critical, and deliberate about what, when, and how to integrate technologies. This critical selectivity is a really valuable skill to model to our students. It will help to ensure that technology integration remains purpose-based and manageable in the long run.

Step 4: Troubleshoot and Try It Out

We know how busy a school day can be, but we cannot stress enough the importance of giving yourself time to try out the technology to be used in the lesson, especially while you are getting started with this new approach. Give your lesson a quick test run, ideally in the room you will use, with the exact technology you plan to use in the lesson. If you have a person within your school that is responsible for the technology, or who is also integrating technology in their classroom, consider going over your lesson with that colleague. They may be able to help identify areas of the lesson that could be troublesome and suggest solutions.

As you test the lesson, think through the flow and chunks of the lesson both as a teacher and from the perspective of your students. Where might students need extra time—during logging in, connecting devices, or playing and exploring? Look for points where problems may occur or a portion of the lesson where you feel the least confident. Is the problem related to overestimating student prior knowledge and skill or is it more of an infrastructure problem that concerns you? How can you avoid the problem? Whom can you ask for help prior to the lesson? Consider ways to troubleshoot problems that may arise.

Before you feel confident with troubleshooting problems during a lesson, we encourage you to have a simple backup plan in mind that can be used in the case of an absolute technology breakdown. The alternative lesson may be going back to that original learning engagement idea identified in step 2 of the process, or it might be something totally different, but just knowing you have an alternative will give you confidence and peace of mind. As we discussed in Chapter 3, sometimes lessons just don't go as we planned, whether or not we are using technology, and if you run into problems during your lesson, try to do what you would normally do in these situations: pause or stop, move on, and come back to it later when the problem is solved.

As you integrate technology more and more in your teaching you will naturally learn to troubleshoot common problems without needing to make contingency plans, just as your ability to do this in other lessons and subjects has grown as you have become a more experienced teacher. As you go through the process of troubleshooting lessons in your planning, you will learn and transfer this knowledge to future lessons. Troubleshooting will become easier and less time-consuming as it becomes embedded in your practice. There is often a misconception among teachers that there are teachers who are good at teaching with technology and teachers who are bad at it. This is not the case: there are teachers who are more or less confident with technology, who have developed more or less resilience for rolling with the punches technology can sometimes throw, or who are more or less open to making themselves vulnerable with technology and learning from mistakes. Anyone can learn to be good at teaching with technology if they give themselves the time. Take the time; it is worth it.

Troubleshooting Common Technology Issues

Unreliable Internet Connection	<ul><li>Download videos or audio to use with students in advance.</li><li>Use apps or software that works offline.</li><li>Record videos, photos, products on the device (e.g., in the camera roll) during lessons, but upload to an Internet-based platform (e.g., digital learning journal) after class or school, when the Internet is under less pressure.</li></ul>
Stressful or Time-Consuming Login Process for Students	<ul><li>Practice logging in and out of devices with students several times when not under pressure to teach or do a project.</li><li>Log devices in for students before the lesson, if time is short or students are too young to log in independently.</li><li>Consider assigning devices to students to reduce sign-ins and raise accountability.</li><li>Speak to technical support staff about the possibility of using a single-sign-in service in the future.</li></ul>
Difficulties Displaying Images or Playing Sound on Classroom Displays	<ul><li>Check presentations and audiovisuals before lessons.</li></ul>

Difficulties Accessing Websites	» Check that websites are accessible at least a few days before the lesson, and make sure that they work.
	» Try doing everything you will ask your students to do, in school, on a school device. Some websites work with some browsers better than others, and some may have been inaccurately flagged as inappropriate in school security systems, meaning they might work in your house or even on your teacher computer but not for students. If you encounter difficulties, contact technical support.
General Problems with Devices or Software	» Try googling the issue. If you describe the problem clearly, often an answer will come up!
	» Ask colleagues if they have had the same problem and know how to solve it.
	» It might sound silly, but check whether everything is plugged in and present. Sometimes cleaning or technical staff might unplug or move something and forget to put it back or notify you that there has been a change.
	» Contact your technical support team for advanced help.

Figure 6.3

When you are beginning, the success of the lesson is greatly dependent on student learning and your level of frustration. Thinking through possible problem areas ahead of time will decrease your anxiety and help support your understanding of the technology you'll be using. Figure 6.3 lists some ways to handle common technological problems.

Step 5: Live the Learning

Here is the moment when you take that deep breath and go for it! Whether you have been planning for a single lesson or a project, prior to this moment you may have discussed the lesson or project with your students, explained or explored the core learning, provided the students with time to explore and play with the technology tool, and shared with the students how you have planned to integrate technology in this lesson. Consider letting your students know if you are also unfamiliar with the tool you will be using: learning with your students facilitates an open and collaborative learning environment, and you may find they are more than capable of helping if you or other students run into problems.

Technology Teaching Tip

Always be clear with your students what your expectations are for their behavior when using technology. Many teachers make the mistake of thinking that if they don't mention how a tool could be misused, the students won't figure it out themselves. We can assure you they definitely will!

Students generally know how they are expected to behave in class (because you and many other adults have told them), but sometimes the novelty of a digital tool can undermine these behavioral norms. To avoid this, think ahead about how you expect students to use the technology and how you do not wish them to use it. Make it clear to students that digital behavior is simply behavior: that means relating examples of digital behavior to acceptable classroom behavior and being consistent with the consequences you apply for misbehavior. Students understand that shouting out random silly phrases during class is not acceptable; neither is it acceptable to type nonsensical or irrelevant messages on a shared digital platform. Students know that passing notes in class is not acceptable; neither is AirDropping or emailing photos to other devices without permission. Likewise, students would never dream of taking another student's notebook and throwing it in the bin; explain that doing this with a digital document is exactly the same and will have the same consequences. If you expect students to use proper spelling, punctuation, and grammar in online comments rather than text speak, make that clear to them at the outset. As you become more experienced with teaching with technology, you will become more familiar with the potential issues and better able to head them off before they occur. Also, as technology becomes a common tool in your classroom, it will cease to be a novelty, and your students will learn what the expectations are for its use just as they understand your expectations for their behavior at all other times.

As you move through the phases of your planned lesson or project, do so with a watchful, reflective eye. Take notes and document your thoughts, and capture student learning and collaboration, all of which will support your process of reflection after the lesson. The following questions may be a starting point for note-taking during the lesson:

1. Was the lesson or project introduction focused on the core learning?

2. Are the planning and scaffolding meeting the needs of the students?

3. Is the progression of the lesson supporting student learning and gradual release of responsibility?

4. While the students may be enjoying the technology tool, are the students on a process of learning connected to the outlined core learning for the lesson?

5. Are there aspects of the lesson that will need to be revisited?

6. What aspects of the lesson allow for continuation in future lessons?

When living the learning, you will naturally be monitoring student learning, motivation, and engagement, among the many other aspects teachers observe. However, when living a lesson that includes technology integration, we advise you to be mindful of one other major consideration: Is the technology overpowering the content or purpose of the lesson? Technology use can be exciting—and there is nothing wrong with students enjoying a lesson! However, it is important that we look critically at whether the technology's integration in the lesson brings only enjoyment or whether it also fulfills its primary purpose of extending or enhancing student learning or allowing for the application of the intended skills or understandings.

Step 6: Reflect to Support Teaching Development

Reflection is easy to overlook in the hectic, ever-changing day of a teacher. But we truly believe that even five minutes of mindful reflection is worth every minute, so try to plan it into your day. As you reflect on the lesson, there are two valuable parts to evaluate: the effectiveness of the lesson as a whole and the effectiveness of the technology integration in meeting the purpose of that lesson and contributing to student core learning. You will probably have many feelings upon completing that first lesson integrating technology in a new way. Initially you may feel that the lesson all around went well, you may feel the lesson was a failure, or you may feel somewhere between those two extremes. Odds are that as you begin to engage in reflective thought, you will identify phases of the lesson that were stronger than others. This is all natural and something that we as teachers are not new to.

Following are possible questions to help guide the reflection process. Before you dive into the questions, revisit the lesson's core learning that you outlined at the start of the process (step 1) and the selected assessment (step 2). As you reflect, be clear with yourself about what you are measuring to determine the success of all aspects of the lesson. Is the measurement of success results-based, such as a quiz, or is there a more intangible benefit to the lesson? Not all success can be measured in the short term, and not all student enjoyment is necessarily a sign that a lesson has been a successful learning opportunity.

Effectiveness of the Entire Lesson

- Did the core learning for the lesson remain at the forefront of the planning and learning process? If not, what will you change about the planning or learning process next time?

- Was the learning engagement explicitly connected to the core learning for the lesson? How do you know this?

- Did the chosen lesson assessment task provide an opportunity for students to demonstrate the development of their skills and understandings? If not, what changes would you make to the assessment?

- Was the lesson effectively scaffolded? What would you adjust to be sure the scaffolding supports student learning and agency without overscaffolding?

- How did the level of testing and troubleshooting contribute to the success of the lesson?

- What structures did you put in place regarding the pace and progression of the lesson that allowed students time to extend their current skills level or understanding and connect to the core learning?

As those initial reflections take form, use the following questions to guide the next phase of targeted reflection.

Effectiveness of the Technology Integration

- Did the technology integration support or enhance the core learning, and if so, how?

- Did the technology integration have a role in developing one of the 3 Cs?

- Did the technology integration support student engagement and motivation?

- Did you approach this lesson with an open mindset from the beginning? (See Chapter 3 for more on mindset.) What effect has your mindset had on the success of the lesson?

- Was the time you put into planning for the lesson balanced against the learning or experience that the students got out of the lesson? In other words, was it time well spent?

The last question may be hard to answer at first, but it is a very important one. As we mentioned earlier in this chapter, technology integration has the power to greatly enhance the learning experience for the students, but that doesn't necessarily apply to every lesson. It might be that if the balance of teacher time and energy is not met by student learning, technology integration could be the wrong move for that particular learning experience, or you might need to refine, adjust, or simplify the approach to integration.

And of course, you may choose to develop your own reflection questions. When you give yourself time to reflect in a way that evaluates and informs future practice you will naturally ask yourself questions that will provide for future development and goal setting.

Release of Responsibility and Student Choice

Just as we scaffold the writing process to support a gradual release of writing responsibility to the student, we also need to mirror this process with technology devices, tools, apps, and so on. This generation of students has a higher level of awareness and vocabulary when interacting with technology, but that doesn't directly correlate to their ability to use it effectively to meet a lesson goal. Be conscious of your students' technology skills and understandings, and know that at every level there is the need for scaffolded support.

We believe a successful classroom hosts students who can choose education technologies that meet their purpose to successfully achieve a task. This means that students understand how the technology works and can apply that knowledge when making a decision about what technology to use for a given purpose, rather than choosing a tool purely based on familiarity or other criteria. For example, if a student chooses to use word-processing software for a presentation, is that tool truly the best choice in terms of features and applicability for the purpose in question, or would another tool perhaps be more user-friendly and more suitable? In order to support students' ability to make these choices, teachers need to scaffold the choice-making process. As you use different education technologies within the classroom, be explicit about why the students will use a particular technology. Be clear about what aspects of this technology support the purpose of the task. Then as students become proficient, provide them with opportunities for structured choice coupled with the articulation of why they made the choice they did.

The Intechgrate Approach to teaching with technology is intended to support the integration of technology through multiple strategies, from self-contained lessons, to embedded integration, to large-scale, multiple-week projects. The approach doesn't change because it is built on strong, purposeful teaching practice. Good teaching is just good teaching, no matter what tools you use! As you walk away from this chapter, keep these key tips in mind:

- *Give yourself time*. Planning for effective technology integration will take additional time. Try to embrace this at first, by maybe planning for technology integration only once a week, but aim to make that learning opportunity as meaningful and connected as possible. If you follow the approach consistently, the time needed to plan, try it out, and trouble-shoot will soon decrease.

- *Be selective*. Strive for quality over quantity. Not every lesson will benefit from technology integration: aim to cultivate a critical selectivity in how and when you integrate technology. This ability to connect purpose, tool, and application is a skill we want to model for our students and help them to develop for themselves as well!

Reflection

- *If your goal is supporting student learning:* Have you planned using all six steps of the Intechgrate Approach to ensure a holistic path to integrating technology? Have you remained focused on the core learning for the lesson? If not, what can you do next time you integrate technology to maintain focus on the core learning?

- *If your goal is supporting professional learning:* What is the most effective way to support teachers beginning to integrate technology using the Intechgrate Approach? How can you use staff meeting or staff development time to support the integration of technology?

- *If your goal is supporting curriculum development:* How does your current curriculum framework support or hinder technology integration?

- *If your goal is supporting systems and structures:* Are there sufficient and appropriate staff and resources in place to support technology integration? Does the staff feel supported to shift practice?

An Integrated Approach to Curriculum

A Guide for Schools

For the vast majority of teachers, written curriculum plays a significant role in how and what we plan and teach. It affects everything we do in the classroom in a way that is so pervasive and so inextricable that sometimes we almost forget to think about it. It can be a little like furniture: necessary, and all around us, but a given and perhaps not something we think deeply or actively about on a daily basis. In this chapter, though, we are going to think about it a lot because understanding and making conscious decisions about how you use your curriculum is extremely important to technology integration. It is where the why of purpose meets the how of pedagogy and gives us the what—what exactly we are trying to teach (and how we will know when students have learned it).

What curricula look like in practice differs in different contexts: from prescriptive and highly specific, to a guiding framework, to general or even vague guidance. Just as variable is the degree to which curriculum is something we, as teachers or even leaders, feel we have influence over. Your curriculum has been developed at the national or governmental level or purchased and provided to you at the state or international level. Alternatively, it might have been developed at the district or school level and be open to review. As teachers we also may feel different degrees of freedom in how we should present the curriculum in the classroom and whether we think of it as being our responsibility to implement, deliver, facilitate, or use as a starting point and adapt.

With awareness of the variety of curriculum styles and approaches around the world, it might seem impossible to say anything about curriculum and technology integration that can apply to all of our readers, but we believe that when it comes to curriculum, and the impact it has on the effectiveness of technology integration, it really is much less about what you have and much more about how you use it.

Believe it or not, it is possible to integrate technology more effectively with whatever curriculum you have, without rewriting it or reinventing the wheel, but to do that you need to take a step back from it and think deeply about what you are truly trying to teach and what might be the optimal way for your students to learn it.

In our experience, finding or being provided with the time for deep, professional dialogue about the purpose of curriculum, its structure, and how we can make the most of the time we have to teach it is rare. More often than not, it seems, the little time we do have to think about curriculum is taken up with the nuts and bolts of the day-to-day planning, teaching, and assessing.

Our hope is that this chapter helps you to find space to think about curriculum beyond the day-to-day planning and provides a starting point for deeper professional dialogue.

What Is the Written Curriculum?

Written curriculum is usually composed of broad learning goals or standards that are further defined by clearer, more concise learning objectives. The outlined learning objectives may reference knowledge to be acquired as well as skills and understandings to be developed within a particular subject area. You might recognize all or only some of the following features in your own written curriculum:

- progression of knowledge and skills to be acquired by the students
- pacing guide outlining time frames for material to be taught
- assessments (both suggested and required)
- student learning engagements (both suggested and required)
- resources for individual units or lessons
- articulation of vertical alignment of knowledge and skills throughout the grade levels
- assigned responsibility for the teaching material

These features are intended to support the teacher in delivering the outlined curricular material and in some ways to ensure consistency throughout the school system. However, so much of the value of the written curriculum comes from teachers turning these raw ingredients into engaging, powerful, and cohesive learning experiences that develop students' current level of understanding.

The Rationale for an Integrated Approach

Before we go deeper into what an integrated approach is and how you can achieve it, it is important to be clear about why it is essential to take the time and effort required to shift your approach to technology from a stand-alone skill-based discipline to an integrated aspect of learning and teaching.

Preparing Students

If we believe that one of the main purposes of schooling is to prepare students for future opportunities within the global world, then we need to mirror real-world contexts within our classrooms. Technology is not often an isolated aspect of life outside of school. People use technology within their day-to-day lives both personally and professionally to support organization, communication, research, collaboration, and entertainment, among other things. Taking an integrated approach to technology in the curriculum does not mean we don't teach technology skills: it means that to truly prepare students for the unknown future world, we need to decrease isolation and increase connection by emphasizing the use of skills *in context*.

Ensuring Sustainability Within a Fast-Changing World

Technology devices, apps, and tools are changing faster than schools can purchase them. If you think back to what kind of technology was in common use when you were in school, it will become clear that it is impossible to imagine what technologies will be available to our students in just five or ten years. Skill-based technology curricula related to specific technologies significantly shorten the life of the curriculum material and outlined learning. Building curriculum materials based on enduring understandings and transferable learning goals (organization, communication, research, collaboration, citizenship, creation, etc.)

helps to develop a more sustainable approach. Of course, teaching the specific skills for the technology being used within your context has a place, but to make it relevant, transferable, and sustainable it needs to be integrated and applied throughout the wider curriculum.

Making Technology Use Meaningful and Manageable

Taking an integrated approach to curriculum essentially means taking on board the concept that students can learn *about*, *with*, and *through* different subjects, objectives, and tools simultaneously. We don't need to teach first graders a technology lesson on mouse skills and a separate English lesson on illustration. We can address both at the same time by allowing students to learn *about* mouse skills *with* technology *through* creating digital illustrations to a text. We can teach about instructional writing with technology through coding because they both share a common core concept of organization and instruction. We can teach about informational writing and research skills at the same time as teaching students to create high-quality video content.

When we integrate technology into the classroom effectively, meaningfully, and sustainably, we see technology both as a subject in its own right and as a tool that teachers and students use to enhance wider learning. This means that when we are talking about curriculum, we are talking about two separate but, we would argue, fundamentally connected aspects:

- technology-specific curriculum
- general curriculum (English, math, science, etc.)

Most teachers, with the exception of technology specialists, will naturally be focused on the general curriculum, or the curriculum specific to their own specialist subject. If you are in the position of having no technology curriculum or being permitted to redesign the one you have, this may be a daunting prospect, but it is also an exciting one. Later in the chapter we will explore how you can go about planning for, developing, or redesigning a technology curriculum that supports integration. If you are in the position of being supplied with a curriculum that is beyond your control to change, it's likely that you'll still be able to make choices about how to implement that curriculum.

When there *is* a technology curriculum, teaching technology is often seen as the job of the IT teacher or the technology integrator, if there is one. If there is no technology specialist, technology can be seen as an add-on or an unwelcome burden to teachers, who are already at capacity with the demands of the general curriculum.

When we effectively integrate technology, we are teaching technology and other learning objectives *simultaneously*, which shifts the notion of technology from an add-on to a tool that enhances student learning. Creating learning engagements where students are required to integrate technology in a connected, meaningful way also supports the students' understanding of how technology is connected to other areas of their learning.

The aim is not necessarily to teach *more* but to teach *differently*. It isn't possible to make the curriculum smaller or to squeeze more time out of the day, but we can streamline and evolve our approach, letting go of strategies and activities that have served their purpose and replacing them with ones that take advantage of the tools we have and that address the needs of students in the twenty-first century.

A Curriculum Continuum

Taking an integrated approach to your curriculum means looking for commonalities between concepts and goals and finding a balance between the knowledge, skills, and understandings in both general and technology curricula. The balance between technology and the wider curriculum will not necessarily be fifty-fifty at all times.

At times, the explicit focus in a lesson may be on the general curriculum, with technology acting as a support, facilitator, lens, or enhancement, and at other times technology may be the explicit focus while the wider curriculum provides context and application. In Figure 7.1 you can see how the focus for planning and teaching technology and the general curriculum is on a sliding scale, from a strong focus on technology on the left to a strong focus on general curriculum on the right. Returning to the persuasive writing example from Chapter 6, we can see how points 1, 2, and 3 on the curriculum continuum might look in greater detail in Figure 7.2.

Continuum of Planning and Teaching Focus

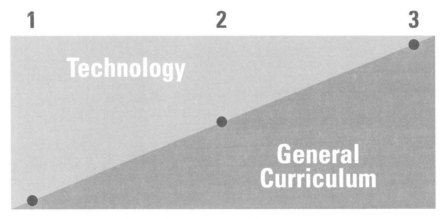

Planning and Teaching Focus

Figure 7.1

Planning and Teaching Continuum Focus Examples

	POINT 1	POINT 2	POINT 3
LEARNING OBJECTIVE	→ Use a variety of filmmaking techniques to create a persuasive digital movie.	→ Use a variety of filmmaking techniques to create a persuasive digital movie that communicates a clearly reasoned and well-supported persuasive argument.	→ Communicate a persuasive argument, supporting claims with clear reasons and relevant evidence.
TEACHING APPROACH	The educator's focus is on teaching the students the necessary filmmaking skills to enable them to produce a high-quality digital product. Persuasion is the context that provides a reason to create the film.	The educator's focus is equally on the product and the purpose or process. The desired outcome is a high-quality movie that demonstrates some or many of the same technical skills as in example 1 but also has a thoroughly explored linguistic and contextual focus. The depth to which the teacher addresses both the technology and the general curriculum outcomes in this example will depend on the time available and the teacher's degree of expertise.	The educator's focus is on teaching the language skills related to persuasion: communication of claims supported by clear reasons and relevant evidence. The movie is only the vehicle for the persuasive argument.

Figure 7.2

continued

PLANNING AND SCAFFOLDING

POINT 1	POINT 2	POINT 3
Planning and scaffolding might focus on exploring camera angles, lighting, on-screen text, music, and sound.	During this phase, the educator might begin with a focus on the aspects of language standards or the goal of persuasive writing. This may involve guiding the students to explore a variety of persuasive texts, identifying features of clear arguments, supporting evidence, and text structure.	Planning and scaffolding for example 3 might begin very similarly to example 2, with increased emphasis on the language skills. The focus is on the language skills related to persuasion, so exploration of exemplars, developing awareness of text and language features, and practice stating and supporting clear, reasoned, and well-evidenced arguments will be of primary importance.
As the context of the movie is not the core learning, the educator might choose to supply the students with a script and storyboard or spend relatively little time on exploring the movie topic.	Next, or simultaneously, the teacher might introduce students to a selection of the technical features of films.	Once the students are confident with the language skills, the educator may choose to introduce digital movies as the means they will use to convey their arguments. Limited time may be spent introducing the chosen movie-making tool and ensuring the students are able to use its key features, but filmmaking techniques are unlikely to be directly taught.
Skills related to persuading the audience may be limited to the impact of technical elements such as lighting, music, pacing, or framing.	Finally, the students will create their own persuasive movies. They will tie together their language and technology learning experiences and apply them to a relevant context to create their movies.	

Figure 7.2

continued

ASSESSMENT

POINT 1	POINT 2	POINT 3
The degree to which the students have achieved the learning objective will be assessed primarily on the technical merits of the movie. The rubric or grading system will be based on the filmmaking features explored during the planning and scaffolding phase. Assessment of the persuasive argument itself will be, at most, limited.	At the end of this learning experience, the students will be assessed equally in two regards: the degree to which they created a high-quality movie and the persuasiveness of that movie based on the formation of a clear argument that's well supported by evidence.	Assessment here focuses on the persuasive argument conveyed by the film. The educator might assess the written script and look for the features of language and persuasive argument taught during the learning experience, such as structure, tone, and evidence. The teacher will either not assess the quality of the movie itself or assess it to a significantly lesser degree.

Figure 7.2

You might notice that even though students from all three examples end up creating a persuasive movie, the teacher's explicit planning and teaching focus shifts along the continuum, altering the specifics of the process, the outcome, and the assessment.

In example 1 we see that the teacher's focus is primarily on the technology skills inherent in making a movie: the filming, lighting, camera angles, and editing process. Persuasion here acts as context, providing the students something to make a movie about, while the direct teaching is focused on technology-specific outcomes. In example 3, that focus has shifted away from technology as the *end* and it becomes more the *means*: the movie is just the vehicle for the students to communicate and demonstrate what they have learned about persuasion from their language curriculum. In the middle sits example 2, which aims to teach both technology skills and language skills in equal measure. As you might imagine, this is the approach that takes the most conscious effort on the part of the teacher and the longest to complete as a process. This approach requires the teacher to plan in such a way that they deliberately teach the knowledge, skills, and understandings from both curriculum standpoints along a timeline that moves the students progressively through the process, providing purpose for their learning.

Learning to think about and implement curriculum in this way does require a shift in thinking and in approach, and as we suggested in Chapter 6, at the outset it may take longer to plan for than the approach you may be used to. However, with growing awareness of and familiarity with the commonalities and possibilities existing between all aspects of the curricula within your context you will find that this new way of planning and teaching will become second nature and a natural evolution of your existing teaching practice.

A Technology Curriculum at the Classroom Level

But what if you don't have a specific technology curriculum, or you have one that is outdated? Being able to design a technology curriculum of your own can be a wonderful, if perhaps daunting, opportunity about which we go into more detail in the coming section. If this is not something you can take on at a school level, you can still decide for yourself what you believe is important for your students to know, understand, and be able to do with technology. To do this, draw on the same approaches and resources you might apply to building a technology curriculum (see next section), but apply the process in your own classroom. If you're working with an unwieldy, unhelpful, or out-of-date technology curriculum, you might use the same process: look at the articulated outcomes and think about how they contribute to the bigger picture of technology concepts and applications (see Figure 7.3).

The table in Figure 7.3 is by no means exhaustive: in your own technology curriculum you may find many technology-specific skills not listed here. There will always be technology knowledge, skills, and understandings that you will need to teach explicitly, but it is our belief that most aspects of all curricula benefit greatly from being taught and applied in context. Context helps our students see the relevance and meaning in what they learn, and it helps them transfer and apply that learning more widely in the future. As students get older and some technology skills and understandings become more sophisticated, it makes sense to rely more on specialist technology teachers to teach them. However, aspects of the technology curriculum such as citizenship, research skills, evaluation and creation of media and content, and digital collaboration will be accessible even to nonspecialists, and that is where an integrated approach to curriculum comes into play.

While your technology curriculum plays an important role, your approach to implementing it has the ability to be a game changer. It's important to reiterate that when it comes to technology, it is not so much about what you have, but about how you choose

Moving from Skill-Based Objectives to Application-Based Objectives

STAND-ALONE SKILLS	DEEPER CONCEPTS	INTEGRATED APPLICATIONS
Mouse skills (e.g., right- and left-clicking)	Creation	Using mouse skills to create digital illustrations
File management (e.g., saving, naming, and organizing files and folders)	Information or organization	Using keywords to name and locate information (e.g., research)
Typing	Communication	Typing while meeting language objectives, such as writing letters or essays, taking notes, making lists, contributing to newsletters or blogs
Email composition	Communication	Using emails to practice using appropriate tone, addressing a specific audience, or contacting curriculum-linked authors, public people, or experts
Internet Safety Day	Communication or digital citizenship	Placing an ongoing, day-to-day emphasis on building empathy, communicating respectfully, using digital comments to communicate helpful peer feedback, and reflecting
Coding	Organization, algorithmic thinking, problem solving, or creating	Exploring instructions and instructional writing as approaches to algorithmic thinking, debugging as a form of problem-solving, or creating games, music, or solutions to problems connected to the wider curriculum

Figure 7.3

to use it—and this is equally true of curriculum. Just as educators recognize the power in learning *about* language by learning *through* language, an integrated approach to technology in the wider curriculum can harness that same power.

A School-Wide Technology Curriculum

If you are in a position to have more ownership over the development, revision, or design of a technology curriculum specifically for your context (whether that context is a district, a school, or your own classroom), then you are in a wonderful position to articulate one that supports an integrated approach to learning and teaching. However, like many wonderful opportunities, it can also be overwhelming. To help guide you through the process, we outline our suggested phases of designing and developing an integration-focused technology curriculum. Bear in mind this is not a prescriptive process: you will need to pick and choose elements that make sense in your context and adapt them to suit your specific need.

As previously stated, within an integrated technology curriculum, the focus shifts away from teaching skills for skills' sake to teaching students to apply skills in a broader context. Instead of asking students to learn to type, save documents, or code for the explicit purpose of knowing how to do those things, we structure the curriculum in such a way that these kinds of skills are primarily developed as a consequence of using technology in context. We start by asking a broader question about what and how we want our students to learn *in general* and then consider which technology skills will be most valuable for our students in achieving that goal.

In Figure 7.3, we listed some common stand-alone technology skills and demonstrated how these can instead be thought about by concepts and purpose. When designing an integrated technology curriculum, begin with broader concepts and purposes such as these, which you believe are most valuable to learning in general and support the broader curriculum, and then consider which skills students will need to meet them.

How you structure this will depend a great deal on the specifics of your context. In some countries, there are specific technology tools and skills that must be taught or that cannot be used, depending on government guidelines. In some schools, programs such as the International Baccalaureate (IB) suggest to a certain degree how such a curriculum should be structured (e.g., under the six Primary Years Programme Information Communication Technology Skills). Beyond such constraints and guidelines, we would recommend structuring your curriculum in the same way as most written curricula are structured.

1. *Learning goals*: These are broad statements about the intended learning that should take place.

2. *Learning objectives*: These are narrower statements that break down what the students should specifically learn to do in order to meet the learning goal.

3. *Skills and competencies*: These are the skills that the students will need to develop in order to be able to meet the learning objective.

4. *Application*: What should teachers do in the context of the wider curriculum that will enable them to teach these goals, objectives, and skills?

To provide you with an example of how this might look, we have drawn from the 2016 ISTE (International Society for Technology in Education) student standards:

- empowered learner

- digital citizen

- knowledge constructor

- innovative designer

- computational thinker

- creative communicator

- global collaborator

As you can see, the intended learning is already framed to support an integrated approach to technology. Using the ISTE standards for students as learning goals and objectives, we can consider which technology-specific and general skills students might need to develop in order to be able to achieve those goals. Following are a few examples.

Knowledge Constructor

- *ISTE learning goal*: "Students critically curate a variety of resources using digital tools to construct knowledge, produce creative artifacts and make meaningful learning experiences for themselves and others."

- *ISTE learning objective*: "3a: Students plan and employ effective research strategies to locate information and other resources for their intellectual or creative pursuits."

- *Possible supporting skills and competencies*:

  › Identify keywords and use them to search for relevant digital resources.

  › Skim and scan nonfiction texts (on- and offline) to identify main points.

  › Take and organize notes when carrying out research, using a variety of tools and approaches.

  › Understand and utilize navigational features on websites and digital tools (menus, navigation arrows, hyperlinks) to find and access information.

- *Possible integrated applications*:

  › Carry out research (independent, supported, or guided, depending on student development) *to inform learning* during social studies lessons or projects.

  › Practice and apply nonfiction text reading skills and note-taking skills *during* research or *as part of* guided reading or language lessons.

Creative Communicator

- *ISTE learning goal*: "Students communicate clearly and express themselves creatively for a variety of purposes using the platforms, tools, styles, formats and digital media appropriate to their goals."

- *ISTE learning objectives*: "6b: Students create original works or responsibly repurpose or remix digital resources into new creations" and "6c: Students communicate complex ideas clearly and effectively by creating or using a variety of digital objects such as visualizations, models or simulations."

- *Possible supporting skills and competencies*:

  › Mouse skills (clicking, dragging, etc.)

  › Typing skills

  › App- or program-specific skills, such as animation or movie creation

  › Planning and organizing ideas to create solutions to problems

  › Coding skills (from algorithmic thinking, to dragging and dropping, to advanced programing languages, iterating and reiterating, and debugging)

  › Aesthetic design skills

- *Possible integrated applications*:

  › Create digital stories with illustrations based on original or existing ideas, depending on age and development.

  › Create a digital product, such as an animation, a movie, or a podcast, to communicate knowledge and ideas (e.g., as a final, summative record of learning).

  › Create a website or digital book to record ongoing learning.

The skills you choose to include in your technology integration curriculum, as well as which structure you choose for learning goals and learning objectives, must depend on the unique circumstances of your students and your context. You might choose to refer to ISTE, the IB, or any number of other international curricula and approaches in gathering together these specifics, a process that we outline in more detail in the coming section.

Things to Consider Before You Start

Teachers strive to be efficient. This is one of our strengths as professionals! But before jumping into the curriculum-writing process, we recommend you take some time to orient yourself and to gather whatever technology curriculum materials are currently or have previously been in place. Make sure you know what is already happening with technology in the school, and look for examples of effective integration and technology teaching that you can build upon.

At times in the process of development it can be easy to forget to acknowledge the impact of work that came before. Even if a curriculum or an approach no longer suits the needs of the students today, it was a valuable point in the development process toward where you now are, just as the work you will do will pave the way for future development. Similarly, there will almost certainly be educators in your context who are already teaching innovatively and creatively with technology, and by building on their examples you can ensure your curriculum has classroom-level support, is rooted in your context, and is not viewed as a top-down initiative.

Writing a curriculum is rarely a solo endeavor; it is the kind of process that really benefits from input, discussion, debate, and varied viewpoints. It can be easy for a single person to miss the gaps in the learning or miss the implications at a resourcing or pedagogical level. Consider forming a group of people to support this process. The specifics of this, again, will largely depend on your context and structures within your school, but in general it might be wise to consider involving the following colleagues if possible:

- curriculum coordinator or leader

- member of the leadership team

- general curriculum educators

- technology specialist

Additionally, consider the benefits of inviting other members of your school community, such as board members, parents, or students, to support and inform at different stages of the process. We encourage you to take advantage of the expertise that teachers bring to the school and collect feedback regarding current practice within the classroom. Involving staff within these processes also supports the development of a shared vision and under-standing and helps create staff buy-in that will support best practice when implementing your technology curriculum.

The Design and Implementation Process

Because of the unique nature of every school and every context, it is not possible (or at least not advisable) to give a list of steps for most processes that will work for everyone—curriculum design included. Please adapt the following considerations to suit your context's and your students' needs.

1. Take Stock of Current Technology Beliefs and Implementation

Every conversation about curriculum should be rooted in the core belief your school has articulated about what is important in learning.

When beginning the conversation about technology curriculum, start with a discussion about your *current* school beliefs regarding technology. These beliefs may be explicitly written within a school mission statement, embedded within school development plans, the school vision, teacher observation expectations, or policies, for example. Or they may not be articulated on paper but are alive within the teaching and learning. What does the way that teachers use and teach with technology reveal about the underlying beliefs about its purpose and importance?

Once you have identified school beliefs, ask: "What is in place to communicate those beliefs to staff? What documentation is in place to support the staff in fulfilling the school beliefs?" It can be easy to assume teachers are all aware of and implementing school beliefs and policies, but over time, as staff come and go and developments lose momentum and visibility, this awareness can be lost.

2. Do Your Research

By this point you may have read and heard a lot about technology integration, but unless you have seen it in action it can be very difficult to conceptualize what it really means and to imagine how it might look in practice. Before going further, get as much inspiration as you can. If you are aware of schools or teachers outside your own immediate context who are integrating technology innovatively, creatively, or just differently, try to visit or speak with them. Ask about their beliefs, their approaches, and their challenges, triumphs, and recommendations. Looking further, schools around the world are integrating technology in amazing ways, and social networks like Twitter are an amazing resource for connecting with teachers and schools who can inspire and inform the next stages of this process.

In terms of written curriculum, there are national and international examples of technology curricula that can provide excellent source material from which to draw. Even curricula with which you disagree are useful as they give you ideas of what you want to avoid and how you would like your own curriculum to be different. Schools, districts, and state curricula are often shared online. As starting points we would recommend the following:

- Scotland's "Curriculum for Excellence: Technologies: Experiences and Outcomes"
  https://education.gov.scot/Documents/Technologies-es-os.pdf

- "The Australian Curriculum: Technologies"
  https://www.australiancurriculum.edu.au/f-10-curriculum/technologies/

- "ISTE Standards for Students"
  https://www.iste.org/standards/for-students

- "The Role of ICT in the PYP" (IB Primary Years Programme)
  https://www.aischool.net/pdfs/Scopes%20and%20Sequences/ICT%20
  IB%20PYP.pdf

Engage in professional discourse, and read articles and publications from organizations that are working to support technology integration, such as ISTE, the IB, and Project Zero (Harvard University), as well as academic publications (Google Scholar is a good, free resource). By collecting and critically analyzing as much information as you can, you will arm yourself with a well-rounded knowledge base on which to build a technology curriculum that's appropriate for your school.

Also, don't underestimate the value of what may be happening already in your own school. Every school and every teacher, whether they are aware of it or not, has been on a continuous journey of working with technology in the classroom. Through this journey a lot has been learned, and there may be teachers in your school who are already doing some great things. Look out for teachers who are

- experimenting with or exploring different digital tools;

- incorporating technology into lessons;

- working with colleagues to evaluate what might be best;

- using technology as a teacher tool to support learners; or

- interested in and reading about technology within the classroom.

Investigate and collect what is already going well within your context, and use this as a base to build from. By looking for a natural continuation point within your context, you are placing value on the work your staff has done to get to where the school is at the moment.

3. Define or Refine Your Vision of Technology Integration

Having taken stock of your school's current beliefs regarding technology and technology integration, you are now in a position to consider whether and how you need to develop that vision.

The clarification and articulation of the school's broader beliefs about technology's role and purpose in life and in education are important precursors to defining a vision for technology integration. These wider beliefs are really the why of technology: Why is it important for students to have access to and to learn to use technology meaningfully in their education? Why does technology matter beyond school, and what are your beliefs about what its role is and should be, now and in the future? Specifically, how might *your* students benefit from using technology as a tool to enhance their learning?

From this big-picture *why* you can then articulate a *how* of technology integration: How will your teachers and students use technology to enhance learning in a way that supports big-picture technology beliefs?

To make your vision of technology integration as concrete as possible, imagine walking around your school and seeing your ideal technology integration in action. What do you imagine seeing in the classrooms? How would students of different ages be engaged in using technology? What would the teachers be doing? How might the teachers be feeling about technology? How would what was happening enhance teaching and learning?

From here, try to articulate this vision in a way that can eventually be shared with teachers and the wider community; all the work involved in developing your curriculum will be for nothing if nobody understands the ultimate goal or why it is so important!

4. Focus on Your Students

Having gathered a wide range of information and impressions about technology curricula and technology integration, now is the time to narrow back in on your own context and the core purpose for all of this: the students.

There is no objectively right or wrong answer about what aspects of technology are most important for students of any age to learn. Many people, for example, consider learning to code to be a vitally important skill for the future, while just as many others vehemently disagree and argue that problem-solving is more valuable. There is no way to know for sure what knowledge, skills, and understandings our students will benefit most from in the future; all we can do is explore options and carefully consider what we believe to be the needs of *our* students.

Which elements, from your research, do you consider to be most important for your students (computing skills, coding, creative expression, digital citizenship, STEM, etc.)? You might identify several areas that are not currently being explored or taught in your context, and if it seems that there are too many to introduce at once, you are probably right! Think about the development of the curriculum in phases: In the immediate short term you might aim to lay strong foundations with a purpose-based approach to integrating the technology you have in place right now, focusing on technology knowledge, skills, and understandings that are meaningful, relevant, and attainable. In the medium term and long term, you can build on this foundation by adding new elements to the curriculum, along with new technologies (if necessary) to the classrooms and school, when teachers and students are ready to go further.

You will get to the specifics of what exactly you want students to learn in the coming stages, but at this point the goal is simply a broad agreement on what elements you should include in your technology curriculum.

5. Gather Feedback from the Community

Depending on how you have structured your curriculum development group (if you have one), you may already have ongoing insight into how the wider school community feels about the development process so far. If not, however, now may be a good time to check in with the school community and various stakeholders, such as teachers, technology specialists, parents, students, administration, and the school board.

In order to successfully implement the curriculum and build on it in the future, it is important that the school community is aware of it, understands it, and feels that its opinions, reservations, and previous contributions have been heard and appreciated. This is a very valuable opportunity for you, too, to assess the current mindset around technology and to begin to consider what professional development and support may be necessary to enable teachers to use the curriculum effectively once it is developed.

6. Create a Plan and Assign Areas of Responsibility

By this point in the process you will have amassed quite a lot of information and ideas, and you will have a vision of the role you believe technology integration should play in your context along with a general agreement of what aspects of technology you feel are important for your students to learn.

Armed with that information, now you can begin the challenging but rewarding work of making your vision as specific and clear as possible. Do this by articulating what students should know, understand, and be able to do after progressing through your curriculum. You should consider the following questions.

What age range will the curriculum cover?

Is your curriculum intended for elementary, middle, or high school, or is it meant to provide a cohesive and progressive continuum across two or more age ranges?

How could you structure the curriculum?

For your overarching structure you might choose to draw inspiration from one of the resources mentioned in step 2 (e.g., the IB PYP's "Role of ICT in the PYP," which suggests six transferable skills, or the ISTE Standards for Students, which are organized under seven headings). Different structures will form the basis for very different outcomes, and you should think carefully about whether the structure you choose supports or undermines the vision you have for technology learning and integration. For example, structuring your curriculum around very specific or stand-alone skills (e.g., keyboard skills and coding) is likely to produce a curriculum that is less geared toward integration than one structured around broader or more transferable skills such as creating and communicating.

Where does the emphasis lie?

Is the curriculum focused on knowledge, understanding, or skills? How are these balanced, communicated, and tied to learning goals or learning objectives?

How will it be articulated?

Will there be specific learning objectives for each grade level, or will they be spread out over two or more years?

What is reasonable and realistic?

Trying to do too much too quickly is not likely to be effective or sustainable, so aim for an outcome that is manageable and realistic. Think about your curriculum development in phases: short term, medium term, and long term. Your immediate, short-term curriculum development goal might be to focus on extending, enhancing, or reconceptualizing the ways staff is already using technology in your context to support technology integration at the classroom level. In the medium to long term, you might plan to build on that foundation and introduce new technologies and skills to evolve the level of understanding and application of technology as both a subject and a learning tool.

 With an overall agreed-upon structure in place, create a timeline of what progress you hope to achieve by what time, and assign responsibilities to members of the group (if you have one). Each person involved in writing the curriculum should ideally have a clear responsibility and goal, along with a time frame in which to accomplish it before you will all come back together to synthesize your work so far.

7. Draft, Synthesize, and Gather Feedback

It's time to get writing! Whether you are doing this alone or as part of a team, writing can be a challenging yet rewarding process. The way in which you will manage your writing process depends a great deal on the specifics of your role and your context and the resources (in terms of time and space) available to you. You may be lucky enough to have dedicated time and space in which to work on your draft curriculum, or you may be snatching time where you can, which will affect how long the process takes.

If you are working as a development group, you'll need to come together to exchange, compare, and synthesize the writing you have done so far. Consider whether it is consistent in terms of the points listed in step 6, in tone and in style. It is very important at this stage to look for gaps and overlaps: do the knowledge, skills, and understandings contained in your curriculum build on each other in a way that is continuous, progressive, and cohesive?

Some redrafting may be necessary at this stage, but once a completed draft curriculum exists, it is very important to get feedback from the people who will be tasked with using it. Share it with those teachers, and possibly even the wider community, and give them time and encouragement to examine the curriculum with a critical (yet ideally constructive) eye. Ask for feedback about these elements:

- *Clarity*: Is what you are expecting the teachers to teach and the students to learn clear?

- *Manageability*: Is the curriculum a manageable size? Are you asking teachers to cover too many objectives in too short a time?

- *Resources*: Are the resources the curriculum demands really accessible, reliable, and in place? If not, what needs to be done?

- *Support*: What training do the teachers feel they may need in order to be able to deliver this curriculum effectively?

- *Vision*: Does the curriculum support the vision for technology and technology integration you communicated at the beginning of this process?

Gather the feedback and consider it objectively before making changes and redrafting. Which feedback do you need to act on to make the curriculum effective and to ensure as much community buy-in as possible?

8. Implement, Sustain, and Embed

The word *implementation* is often used as though it is a single action: an initiative is created, and then it's implemented (introduced, rolled out, published, etc.), and what happens in the classroom changes. In fact, developing anything about teaching and learning is an involved process. Implementing a curriculum successfully requires much more than simply announcing that it is finished and expecting everyone to get on with it; initiatives that are "implemented" in this way tend not to stay implemented for very long!

The real challenge with any initiative is in providing the support and creating the structures necessary to ensure that the implementation of the initiative is sustained in such a way that it becomes an embedded part of how teachers teach and students learn in the long term. During the implementation phase, be aware of the following elements.

Mindset and training

Central to ensuring your curriculum implementation is sustained and embedded is considering what support teachers will need in order to implement the curriculum in the classroom successfully. As we explored in Chapter 3, teachers' mindsets will play a key role in determining the degree, the willingness, and the efficacy with which they'll implement the curriculum you have created. You may already be aware of a range of technology training needs among your teachers, but this may be a good opportunity to find out what training they feel they will need to be able to bring your curriculum to life in the classroom. One option might be to conduct a survey (Google Forms is an excellent, free resource for this) to find out how confident teachers feel in using the technologies and teaching the learning objectives outlined in your curriculum and use this as a basis for providing needs-based training. In Chapter 3 we also discussed the features of effective professional development. Think carefully about what options you have for providing differentiated, needs-based, classroom-focused training so that you are teaching your teachers in the same high-quality way you ask teachers to teach their students. You might consider modeling, coaching, peer-mentorship, and small-group differentiated support as possible options.

Space for change

At the school level and above, there are always many priorities for development such as assessment, language, and differentiation. The existing priorities will never cease to be important, but not everything can be a priority at once. If the implementation of the technology curriculum is going to become a priority on which teachers should focus, something else will need to move aside, even temporarily, to make space for it. We cannot simply keep adding more to the metaphorical plate of teaching without something falling off or becoming a token add-on.

At the classroom level, rolling out a plan at a staff meeting will take a technology integration curriculum only so far. Once that meeting is over, the existing daily demands of the job once again tend to become a teacher's natural priority. Asking teachers to evolve and develop their use of technology in the classroom will require regular reinforcement and refocusing so that it remains a conscious, visible, and explicit goal in the classroom even as these demands continue to compete for attention. Planning ahead to make dedicated time and space for regular conversations about technology teaching and integration, whether that is through whole-staff meetings, team or grade-level discussions, or some other mechanism, will help teachers to remain focused on the goal and reassure them that the effort they will need to invest in the process is valued and valuable in the long term.

Clarity of expectations and goals

Every faculty is different, and in some contexts there is greater openness to change and development than in others. It may be that simply introducing the curriculum and providing support will mean that all the teachers in your context will take it on board and run with it, or it may be that some or several will take a more relaxed approach or seek to opt out entirely. Only the leadership team in each context can assess and decide the degree to which they need to put in place concrete expectations about the rate and degree of curriculum adoption and how they will do it. In general, some of the following approaches may be helpful:

- Set predetermined, transparent whole-staff check-in points to discuss and share progress and practice.

- Transparently and deliberately look out for and discuss technology integration and teaching during teacher observations and assessments.

- Embed technology-related goals into professional goal-setting cycles.

- Look for, celebrate, and share examples of technology teaching and integration with the school community in the newsletter, weekly memo, or blog.

9. Review, Refine, and Redraft— Repeatedly!

No curriculum is ever truly finished. Every curriculum should be subject to regular review and refinement as part of the implementation process: what we know about learning and what we believe is important for our students to know, understand, and be able to do change over time. Nowhere, arguably, is this more the case than with technology.

Technology itself changes at an incredible rate: as your infrastructure and resources are replaced or updated, the curriculum will need to shift to take those changes into account. More importantly, as your and your staff's understanding and beliefs develop about how you can and should use technology to enhance learning, so must the curriculum, which is simply the written expression of how technology should be used in the classroom to support that belief.

Developing how technology is integrated and taught is a journey at every level—it's a journey for the teachers and a journey for schools too. We do not, and cannot, expect teachers to change how they use and teach technology overnight or to change permanently and perfectly: refinement and review is necessary and healthy.

The timing and extent of the reviewing, refining, and redrafting process may depend to a degree on the extent to which the approach to technology teaching and integration, and the curriculum itself, has changed during this process. For some contexts, the developments might constitute a tweak, while in others they may represent a complete pedagogical or ideological shift. The greater the development, the longer and more involved the review process may need to be. Whatever the timeline and structure of the review process you decide upon, it should ideally be transparent and clearly communicated to the school community from the outset. This will make clear to staff not only that the school is on a journey just as they are but also that the experiences and challenges they have while implementing their new curriculum will be productive in contributing to the review process.

Review

Review can take two major forms: (1) informal and ongoing and (2) formal. If you are situated in the school or context where the curriculum is being implemented, it will be possible to gather ongoing, informal feedback about the curriculum from the teachers using it, through conversations or planning or team meetings. What aspects are they finding challenging? Are gaps and overlaps emerging? Where are problems arising with resources and infrastructure or with the relationship to the general curriculum? What is working well? If possible, observe the curriculum in action: How is it working for students? What are the next steps?

In addition to gathering ongoing feedback, you might have a formal review at the end of the first or second academic year of implementation. You could ask the same questions through a survey or during a school meeting to inform the next stage.

Refine

In the medium term, approximately two to four years into implementation, hopefully it will not be necessary to make major redrafts to the curriculum. Instead, using the feedback from the review process, you might make refinements by adding, removing, or altering learning objectives, accounting for new resources or infrastructure that have been introduced, or reconsidering specific skills.

Redraft

The time will probably come when the needs of the students, the capacity of the teachers, or the technology in the school (resources and infrastructure) has developed to such an extent that a full redraft of the curriculum will be necessary or desirable. Once your curriculum has been in place for five years, this may be a good point at which to begin asking yourself and your teachers whether this is the case. The good news is that when you get there, you will have a sound foundation on which to build, the feedback and involvement of your school community over the review and refinement phases, and experience of how to build a technology curriculum to fit your context!

Reflection

- *If your goal is supporting student learning:* What transferable skills are currently outlined within your technology curriculum? Do you feel they are clearly articulated for application within the planning and teaching process?

- *If your goal is supporting professional learning:* What support or training would your staff need to engage in a curriculum-development process?

- *If your goal is supporting curriculum development:* What aspects of your current technology curriculum support an integrated approach to technology skills and understandings? What aspects of your curriculum do not?

- *If your goal is supporting systems and structures:* Do the systems and structures within your school support or hinder the implementation of your current technology curriculum?

Resources, Systems, and Infrastructure

08

A Pedagogical Approach

hether you are a teacher or a school leader, you may be reading the title of this chapter and thinking, "What has that got to do with me?" and preparing to skip ahead. Hopefully we have caught you before you have moved on, because this chapter has *everything* to do with you!

As we wrote at the very start of this book, technology integration is an educational discussion, and as educators we have a right and a responsibility to be a part of the whole discussion to ensure that technology is being resourced, supported, and implemented in schools in a way that enhances teaching and learning. We recognize that systems and infrastructure are the part of a school that teachers and even leaders may have the least control over; decisions and budgets are often set at the national, state, or district level, which individual schools have very little, if any, control over. However, our aim in this chapter is to provide you with a prompt and a framework to actively consider how systems and resources are working in your context and to encourage you to use your voice in asking for and suggesting change when it is needed.

Why Resources, Systems, and Infrastructure Matter

Picture a building—it could be a house, a school, a museum, a shop, or any building you are familiar with. On the superficial level are all the things about a finished building that you can see: the visible structure, the style, the interior decoration, the furniture, and so on. When the building functions well and meets its purpose, these tend to be the elements of a building that we all focus on because they are immediately tangible. But long before that building was completed, many more considerations were put in place during the construction process. The architectural vision, the blueprints and building design, the construction project management, the skill of the people involved in the build, and the foundations and beams that act as the fundamental load-bearing structure were all crucial in creating and supporting the final, visible level or finished building.

Technology integration is like that building: on the surface level are all the visible resources that we use on a day-to-day basis. The student and teacher technologies like desktop computers, tablets, robots, and interactive whiteboards and resources like apps and subscriptions to websites are like the interior decoration and furnishings of a building: they are eye-catching, and we use and are aware of them on a daily basis. Often when we judge a school on its technology, whether as teachers, students, or parents, we are considering this level: how much technology does it have; how up-to-date is it; does it have a makerspace? Whether or not any of these aspects work to enhance teaching and learning, however, depends very much on those other, crucial elements: simply buying robots or providing a device for each student and teacher is not going to create the conditions for effective technology integration, just as buying lots of chairs and tables and leaving them on a building site will not create a successful restaurant!

One of the crucial elements that determines the success of a building is the vision that defines it: what is the building's purpose? A house that is designed on the same scale and style as a hospital won't be a very comfortable house, and a hospital designed like a house is not somewhere we would want to go to be treated. The purpose is central to informing the plans and the blueprint to construct the building.

Similarly, what is the vision for technology integration in your school? What do you, your colleagues, and your leaders believe about how you should use technology and what role it should play in education? This vision should determine the curriculum, which is the blueprint for technology integration in your context. The role of the leader here is to act as a project manager who guides, supports, sources, and facilitates the implementation of those plans. With the plans and blueprints in place, skilled individuals put the plans into action, whether than means constructing a building or teaching students and integrating technology into their classes.

A key part of ensuring that these plans become a functional building lies in constructing elements that will never be seen: the foundations and the internal structure. Systems and infrastructure are like those core, load-bearing parts of a building: all of the other parts can be in place, but if we don't consider these often-invisible elements, our beautiful building can fall right down. We can see this in schools where technology is available but recurring issues (e.g., Internet reliability or speed, difficulties logging on, lack of device maintenance or replacement) create barriers to technology integration. These issues are more than inconvenient—they fundamentally erode teachers' and students' willingness to integrate and use technology, negatively affecting the curriculum, teaching and learning, and student experiences.

Some Definitions

If you do a search for the words *resources, systems*, and *infrastructure*, you will find various definitions at differing levels of technical specificity, but in this chapter we use them in a more exclusively educationally driven context, as you'll read below.

Our aim in sharing these definitions is to empower you to have conversations with colleagues, leaders, and decision-makers, to give you a voice in identifying what is working well and what is holding you and your students back from utilizing technology at a deeper level. We hope it will help you to be more confident and proactive in suggesting specific changes and improvements when resources, systems, or infrastructure are not supporting technology integration in the way you need them to.

Resources

As in our building metaphor, resources are the surface-level things that we tend to think of when we think of technology:

- teacher devices (desktop computers, laptops, tablets, etc.)
- student devices
- permanent in-class technology (interactive whiteboards, projectors, sound systems, etc.)
- digital subscriptions and software
- additional technology such as robots, circuit boards, and makerspace tools and resources

In addition to things, we can also think of less tangible elements such as staffing positions like specialist technology facilitators or coaches as resources, as well as another crucial resource: money!

Infrastructure

Officially, *technology infrastructure* is used as a collective term for all of the technology in place in an organization: the resources, the people, and the systems. However, when we talk about infrastructure, we are referring specifically to the underlying technical framework that supports the resources in a school:

- Internet access (how the school devices connect to the outside world)
- Wi-Fi (how the school devices connect to the Internet without a cable)
- network (this is distinct from Internet and refers to the way that the computers within a school are connected to each other, rather than to the outside world)
- server (the place where all the school data is stored and the system that essentially controls all the school computers)

A core part of the infrastructure, and one that we as educators rarely see or consider, is physical: the smooth running of these components is reliant on there being sufficient and well-planned cables, switches, Wi-Fi hotspots, network cable plugs, and other equipment that may or may not have been planned for when the building was first made. In older buildings, thick walls can make Wi-Fi less reliable, or a slow network might be partially caused by old cables that were not designed to carry the load that an increased number of devices is creating.

Systems

Again, *systems* can mean lots of different things, depending on the degree of technical specificity, but in this context it means the organizational structures and processes that rely on and utilize the infrastructure:

- core software needed by staff, for example, to take attendance, record grades, and write reports
- the process to request help when a device stops working

- the process for requesting and installing new software or apps on devices

- budgetary planning and ordering of technology resources

Ways to Approach Technology Systems and Infrastructure

In most organizations, technology systems and infrastructure are planned, managed, and overseen by technology specialists, including network administrators and technology or IT directors. This makes sense: large-scale technology is complex and expensive, and it requires specialist knowledge and training to put in place and manage effectively. Understandably, given the skill and training required, it is quite rare (though not unheard of) for the head of the technology department in an educational setting to be a teacher as well as an IT specialist, which means that decisions about technology tend to be driven primarily by technical priorities. Naturally, in an educational setting, the primary goal of all the technology resources, systems, and infrastructure is to support teaching and learning, yet for many schools, it is challenging to establish or sustain an active and strategic collaboration between the technical and pedagogical approaches to technology.

To return to our metaphor, you could imagine this as being somewhat like having two architects managing a project who don't share their plans with each other. One of these architects knows the vision for the project but doesn't involve themselves in the practicalities of its construction, and one designs and builds the structure without fully understanding the purpose of the building. Clearly, this approach would create a building that lacked functionality for its users.

Different schools and contexts have different barriers and systems in place that make it difficult for pedagogical and technical technology leaders and implementers to collaborate. Pedagogical priorities may or may not always align with technical ones, and professionals in both fields (educational and technical) may lack the shared vocabulary and specialist understandings to easily build a working, strategic collaboration. IT departments are often in charge of several campuses or schools, making connecting with the educational vision at the school level a further challenge. Decisions on which resources to buy and implement, or when and whether to go one-to-one and on what platform, may be imposed in a top-down way on multiple schools.

Creating a direct and reciprocal relationship between technical and pedagogical aspects of technology integration may be logistically challenging, but it is educationally important. As we explored in Chapter 3, mindset and teacher beliefs about technology can have a deeply negative impact on implementation and therefore student learning. Unreliable, out-of-date, or user-unfriendly technology is often one of the key factors that makes teachers anxious about using it in their classrooms, and infrastructure that appears not to meet their needs or the needs of their students is a further deterrent against integration. For teachers, purpose is key: if the technology that is in place does not match the educational technology vision for the school, or it fails to support the curriculum, or it is somehow unsuitable, teachers are unlikely to use it in a meaningful way.

As teacher and student capacity and skill develop with the technology that is in place, the curriculum will develop to meet, extend, and capitalize on growing skill and interest levels. This often leads to greater demand for more numerous, more advanced, or more up-to-date resources, which, in turn, places a burden on the systems and infrastructure. When the resources fail to meet pedagogical need, or when an overburdened infrastructure begins to fail or become unreliable, teachers are often advised to scale back on what they are trying to do, effectively restricting their practice to the limitations of the technology. However, if we remember that the purpose of the school is education, and the purpose of the technology is to support teaching and learning, then we have to insist that it is the role of the resources, systems, and infrastructure to keep up with and even anticipate teacher and student need, providing space for skills and understandings to grow, rather than inhibiting and constraining them.

How to Take Action

Unlike in a building, which needs foundations and internal structures in place before construction, if your school has issues at the systems and infrastructure level (and most do), it is never too late to improve them. In fact, ongoing review and improvement of technology systems and infrastructure is a necessary condition for effective technology integration because technology is always changing and developing. It is possible to move forward from a position in which there is a lack of connection between pedagogical and technical approaches to technology and to work collaboratively with vision and purpose at the core of plans and action.

The first step is to objectively consider the technology in your school, whether that is at the whole-school or even classroom level. With a clear overview of the current situation and any issues you have, you will be in a stronger position to begin to identify possible solutions and suggest future developments.

- What resources, systems, or infrastructure are in place at your school that are having a positive effect on teaching and learning?

- Do you, your colleagues, or your staff experience any barriers to technology integration that are created by resources, systems, or infrastructure?

- At what level are those issues—surface resources (things and tools) or at a more fundamental level of systems and infrastructure?

- In an ideal world, what do you think needs to change?

- If you aren't sure what specifically is causing the problem(s), whom could you connect with to get advice?

- What structures are currently in place to enable and encourage communication and collaboration between technical and pedagogical teams beyond reporting technical issues?

- How clearly articulated are your or your school's short-, medium-, and long-term visions for technology use and integration?

In an ideal world, we believe decisions about technology in schools would be made by a team of technical and pedagogical technology specialists who'd collaborate as equals at the leadership level. In many contexts, however, leadership structures are firmly embedded that would prevent this from being easily implemented. Even so, there are many ways that collaboration, shared understanding, and pedagogically based planning can be increased and improved.

Be an Agent for Change

Maximize successes, be aware of barriers, and suggest solutions. Technology in schools is supposed to support and enhance teaching and learning: if it isn't doing that effectively and the problem lies with the technology itself rather than its implementation, then we owe it to our students to address that. We often hear complaints from teachers such as "The Internet is slow." The fact of the matter is that the Internet itself is incredibly fast and truly amazing; if it is slow in your school, there must be a reason for that. Every problem has a solution—we just have to find it! Don't accept fundamental infrastructural issues as inevitable; be an agent for change and advocate for solutions.

Make Connections

Get to know the people who work behind the technology. There can be a tendency for those of us suffering at the hands of ineffectual technology to blame the technicians:

perhaps there are long delays to repairs, or there's a sense that change is too slow. It is very rare, we find, that anybody seeks to do a bad job, and if there are issues with infrastructure is it likely that the technicians are frustrated by those same issues as well. Reaching out to technical IT staff and speaking to them directly about problems and being understanding about the issues they themselves are facing can only help to build relationships and a greater sense of shared purpose.

Beyond your own technical IT team, whom else could you reach out to who is involved in funding, decision-making, or planning that impacts technology integration in your context? Can you use your PLN, whether that is through social media, at conferences, or through visits to other schools, to make connections with helpful teachers, specialists, leaders, entrepreneurs, policy makers, or innovators? Maybe they have inspiring ideas for how to use what you have, how to troubleshoot, or where to go next.

Build Common Understanding

As we have explored, it can be challenging for technical IT staff to have access to and understanding of the pedagogical technology vision at individual schools. Look for ways to be proactive in inviting them into your context to show them what you are currently doing with technology and communicate what you hope to do in the future. Invite them to lend a hand or observe during a lesson that uses technology or to participate in relevant staff training. If you have a technology PLN or occasional workshops, particularly if they are purpose-based, invite them to attend. In this way you can build relationships, help them to access your specialist vocabulary, and develop a common understanding about the purpose behind the technology.

Building common understanding goes both ways, though! The technical staff also have a specialist vocabulary, barriers, frustrations, and plans. Look for ways to learn as much as you can from them to develop your own understanding and you will be better able to collaborate with them as well.

Think Strategically

Naturally, the kinds of changes that are often required when resources, systems, and infrastructure need development are expensive and they take time. It is frustrating for all concerned when time and money are invested in developments that turn out not to be sustainable or cause unintended effects. For example, you may have the issue that you have insufficient devices for your students and want to introduce more laptops or tablets. Many schools do this only to then discover that their Internet or Wi-Fi setup will not cope with so many more devices or that the devices quickly run out of memory. It is impossible to anticipate every possible scenario, but we can aim to look farther down the road than simply solving our current problem. What is the medium- to long-term vision for technology integration in the school, and do you think the changes you are proposing will cover what will be needed five years from now? Do you have the systems and organizational processes in place to manage and maintain these developments?

A collaborative relationship with technical technology leadership will be invaluable during this process, as they will be able to easily spot potential roadblocks and problems that might not occur to education specialists, while the pedagogical vision will fundamentally shape the plans to best suit the specific needs of that educational context.

Focus on Purpose

Above all, do your best to keep educational purpose at the center of discussions, suggestions, and plans. As we discussed in Chapter 6, at times we are all prone to focusing on preference over purpose, and this is true of educators and technicians. The issues we identify and the changes we suggest need to be rooted in our vision for technology integration, at the core of which is student learning. If you, your staff, your colleagues, or the technical IT team are expressing a strong preference for a specific tool, platform, solution, or development, try to encourage everyone to take a step back and ensure that the preference places the student at the center of the decision-making process.

Whether you are a teacher or a leader, there are many components related to systems and infrastructure, and change, as we all know, takes time. You may be facing barriers that are beyond your control right now and that are impacting your teaching and your students.

The question to ask yourself is: What *is* within your control? What resources and infrastructures are in place that you can take advantage of? What leeway and control do you have for short-term change? What would be some steps you could take that would make the most difference for kids? How can you continue to integrate technology while you work on or wait for a permanent solution?

Many teachers and IT specialists feel uninterested or unqualified to involve themselves in the wider aspects of how schools plan for and implement technology. We believe that whatever your role in education, you have skills, knowledge, and understandings that make your contribution to this aspect of how we integrate technology in schools valuable. Whether you are a teacher, a technical specialist, a school leader, or an administrator, we hope that you feel empowered to be an agent for ongoing change by participating in this very important educational discussion and fostering the connections to create a pedagogical approach to resources, systems, and infrastructure within your organization.

Reflection

- *If your goal is supporting student learning:* How can you work with what you have to make the biggest difference to student learning? How articulated are your short-, medium-, and long-term visions for technology integration and implementation? How clearly have you communicated that vision to the IT team responsible for resources, systems, and infrastructure?

- *If your goal is supporting professional learning:* How could you bring IT specialists and teachers together to benefit from each other's knowledge and form a shared understanding of the vision for technology integration?

- *If your goal is supporting curriculum development:* Do the resources, systems, and infrastructure effectively support the skills and understandings you want your students to have with technology?

- *If your goal is supporting organizational systems and structures:* To what extent have the resources, systems, and infrastructure currently in place been planned with the student at the center? What short-, medium-, and long-term changes would appear to make the most difference to teachers and students?

Chapter

09

Leading Technology Integration

Throughout this book we have communicated our belief that effective technology integration requires meaningful vision, deliberate purpose, and thoughtful implementation in multiple areas at once. An exclusive focus on resourcing, or pedagogy, or curriculum, or professional development cannot lead to the integration of technology in a way that truly enhances teaching and learning, because all of these areas are inextricably connected and interdependent.

In Chapter 1 we introduced the Intechgrate Model to illustrate the six key areas that schools must address to ensure technology is integrated and used as effectively as possible to enhance student learning (see Figure 9.1). In the subsequent chapters we explored each element in detail, primarily through the lens of an educator, with discussion, examples of practice, and prompts for reflection. We have emphasized the interdependent nature of these elements and called for a holistic approach to technology integration, listing leadership as one crucial element in its own right. In practice, effective leadership is so important that it is both a discrete element and a vital component of and support to all elements of the Intechgrate Model.

The Intechgrate Model:
A Holistic Approach to Technology in Education

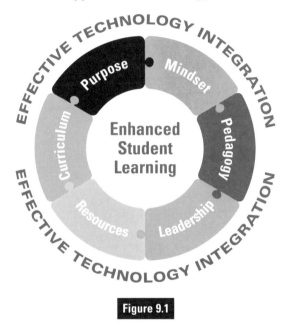

Figure 9.1

Before we explore the role of leadership in technology integration, first we need to consider this question: Who are the leaders in your context, and what is the influence of leadership within your context?

Leadership, and leadership roles, look different from school to school and around the world. From informal teacher-leaders, to middle leaders, to organizational administrators, there will be a range of people in your context who have the drive, vision, influence, and desire to be a part of developing the role of technology integration.

While it is important to identify those in your school who act as leaders, both in a classroom and in an administrative setting, it is equally important to understand the context of their leadership and where they can be most influential. The effective integration of technology calls for those with influence over budgets, policies, and classroom practices to work together. As such, the implementation of a cohesive vision for technology in learning is not a task for one individual: it will require collaborative and distributed leadership and shared vision and purpose by leaders at all levels.

Think about these questions:

- Over which element(s) of the Intechgrate Model do you have influence?

- To what degree and in what way?

- Who else in your context could contribute to the leadership of other aspects of technology integration?

- What steps can you take to begin to build your leadership team and your influence?

Assess the Status Quo

Before undertaking any development, take stock of the current situation and consider the needs, strengths, and challenges that may support or hinder that development. (See Figure 9.2.)

Strengths, Needs, and Challenges

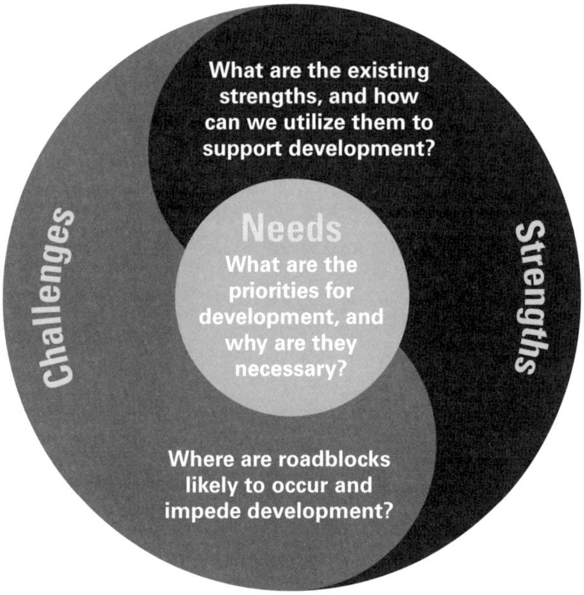

Figure 9.2

Figure 9.3 contains statements to guide and prompt your reflection. Next to each is space to note whether at this time you would consider that element a strength, a challenge, or a need in your context.

Prompts for Assessing the Status Quo, Based on Aspect of Technology Integration

	REFLECTION	STRENGTH, CHALLENGE, OR NEED?
PURPOSE	1. School has a clearly articulated, shared vision or purpose for teaching and learning with technology.	
	2. The vision or purpose puts student learning at the center.	
	3. The vision or purpose encourages the school community to push beyond the familiar to allow for forward-thinking approaches and innovation.	
MINDSET	4. Technology integration is a topic of professional conversation in the school.	
	5. Technology integration is an expectation; that is, it is valued and acknowledged during formal and informal teacher observations.	
	6. Technology professional development takes place regularly in a variety of forms, targeted to teacher and student need.	
	7. The school community, including parents, students, board members, and other stakeholders, are supportive of technology integration.	
PEDAGOGY	8. Professional development actively addresses the effective integration of technology in teaching practices.	
	9. Staff have time to share practice and reflections related to technology integration.	
CURRICULUM	10. The curricula in place (both technology-specific and general) allow for an integrated approach to technology.	
	11. Curricula are reviewed and updated regularly when possible.	
	12. Active and ongoing consideration is given to how the curricula, pedagogy, and vision align to enable effective technology integration.	

REFLECTION	STRENGTH, CHALLENGE, OR NEED?
13. The resources (including human resources), systems, and infrastructure in the school are sufficient, reliable, and aligned with the school vision or purpose for technology.	
14. Effective and active lines of communication exist between leaders and staff members responsible for technology-specific infrastructure, resources, and teaching and learning.	
15. Funds are dedicated to supporting technology integration in an ongoing way.	
16. The funds or funding structures in place are sufficient and sustainable and are aligned with student and teacher needs.	
17. The leadership team, including you, participates in technology professional development alongside other members of staff.	
18. The leadership team is actively aware of their own personal and professional mindsets around technology.	
19. The ongoing development of technology integration is a conscious component of leadership planning.	

RESOURCES

LEADERSHIP

Figure 9.3

Know Your Staff and System Levels

Before we explore in more detail how leadership can best support the development of technology integration, consider the following aspects: your staff and your system levels.

In every school and system, there are staff members who have vision and drive beyond the boundaries of their roles, who can be relied upon to be valuable and effective implementers of the school's developing vision for technology integration. Knowing who these teachers, administrators, and support staff are, as well as having an awareness of who might present barriers to development (deliberately or otherwise), allows you as a leader to make decisions about whom to involve in which ways, whom to trust and rely on, and who may need extra support as the development process progresses.

Additionally, leaders (and their teams) must understand and work within a variety of system levels and processes, both external and internal. Figure 9.4 illustrates how five overarching external system levels, from the school to the international level, exert pressure and influence on the internal development processes outlined in the Intechgrate Model.

At each of these external system levels exist smaller subsystems, and even individuals, which have influence over how development is implemented. For example, at the school system level, you might identify the parent-teacher association, school board, CEO, or teacher working groups as relevant subsystems or individuals.

It is important to articulate what these external systems and subsystems are in your own context, identify their areas of influence, and consider when and how you might best involve them to support deliberate and strategic development of technology integration. Knowing these external system levels, recognizing their relative hierarchy, and understanding how they may drive or even limit internal development processes will help you as a leader to plan for development in a systematic way, with awareness of where you are likely to find barriers and supports. This is particularly important, as to enact lasting and effective change in your school, ongoing development is going to have to take place in multiple areas at once.

In the coming sections, we summarize the core message of each element of the Intechgrate Model, explain how it relates to those in leadership roles, and share our recommendations for ensuring effective and sustainable technology integration.

Purpose

Technology integration's purpose exists at two main levels: the big-picture level (Why does technology integration matter in general?) and the school or contextual level (What does this mean to us, and how should this look for us?). See Chapters 1, 2, 4, and 5 for a more detailed examination of purpose.

The Impact of External Systems on Internal Development Processes

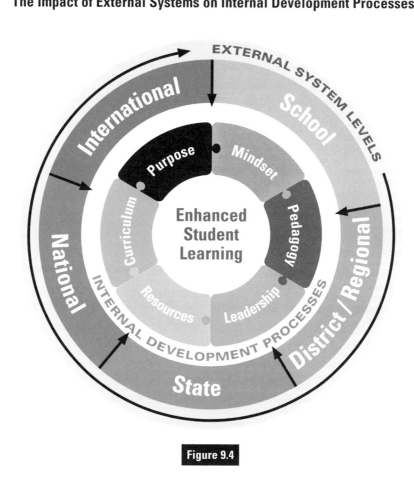

Figure 9.4

Defining and Embedding Purpose in Your Context

Beyond the big-picture question of the purpose of technology in education, it is critical to properly define what the purpose and the role of technology are in *your specific context*. Then you must communicate those definitions to both leaders and other members of the school community. By clearly defining and communicating the role that technology should play in your school, you create a vital bridge between ideology and pedagogy—between what you (as a school) believe about technology's purpose and how you intend that purpose to be realized.

Mindset

For in-depth exploration of the various contextual factors that have an impact on teacher technology mindset—which, studies have shown, is the most influential factor in how effectively technology is implemented—see Chapter 3, page 19.

Assessing Technology Mindset

In Chapter 3 we encouraged teachers to try to be aware of their own individual technology mindsets and the factors that underlie them. Now, we encourage leaders to do the same! It is not hard to be unaware of the influence your own technology mindset can have on the development of technology integration at the school level. If you have concerns or reservations about technology, we encourage you to address them objectively through research (we reference several studies regarding student outcomes and screen time in Chapter 2) and also by simply being aware of your own technology beliefs and mindset. Taking the time to consider their origins is a worthwhile exercise if you hope to help lead the development of technology integration in your school or context.

You may already think that you know how staff in your context feel about technology, but it is nevertheless extremely helpful to take the temperature of technology mindset in the school to find out not just how teachers feel about technology but also *why*. Dedicating a staff meeting or professional development session to exploring this question can be both enlightening and transformative. Teachers are rarely given the time and space to explore questions like this, but if you are going to ask them to be a part of developing how the school uses and integrates technology, it can only help to give them the opportunity to explore their feelings and name their concerns and then consider how you can help them to move forward.

Addressing Technology Mindset

Once you have determined the prevailing technology mindset, moving it forward requires you to figure out which factors are contributing to negative mindsets and then put measures in place to address the factors that are within your control. Technology mindset is a product of a huge array of factors, some of which you may be in a position to address and some of which you may not. No leader can address the aspects of a mindset that arise from a prevailing national or cultural belief about technology or the experiences teachers have had with technology in their personal or professional pasts, but awareness of these will enable you to handle their impact as sensitively as possible.

The factors that you can address are often related to the other parts of the Intechgrate Model:

- purpose

- pedagogy

- curriculum

- resources and infrastructure

- leadership

There are two critical aspects that relate to all of these elements and have a direct and profound impact on teacher mindset: support and training.

Providing effective support and training

Eva Peron is quoted as saying, "Time is my greatest enemy." Perhaps she was a school leader on the side. Training teachers takes time, and there is only a limited amount of that in any school. In contrast, there seems to be an unlimited quantity of priorities a leader is expected to address, using the limited professional development time they have. As with everything else, your context will determine how you organize your professional development time and funding and what the needs of your staff are. With that in mind, we can provide you with some general guidelines for effective staff training with technology.

Atmosphere is important.

Creating an open, supportive community culture around educational technology starts with you and your approach to staff training. Honor the diversity of your staff's varied experiences and levels of comfort with and curiosity about technology. Respect individual needs (strength and challenges), and use them as a way to bring the staff together for the common purpose. Create a culture that invites change at a pace that will work for your staff. The best way we have found to begin creating this culture is through guided professional dialogue both as a whole staff and within smaller working teams.

Be clear about the intention of the support.

Everyone benefits from having time to prepare prior to engaging in meaningful professional dialogue or training. Be clear with staff and share the intention or objective for the training early. This extra time will allow teachers to think, begin conversing, and prepare.

While the specific training needs in your school will be unique, most training and support consists of two general areas:

- *Teacher technology competency*: Support or professional development for teachers' expanding abilities with teacher tools, increasing the teachers' level of comfort, understanding, and overall confidence when working toward integrating technology into their classroom.

- *Teaching and learning*: Support or professional development in planning for, implementing, and reflecting on the effectiveness of meaningful tech integration within the classroom to support student learning and overall development as well as supporting the revision, development, design, or review of curriculum.

Your staff may need to develop in one or both of these areas, but whatever the focus of the training, we have found that one condition remains consistent: differentiated small-group training is almost always most effective.

Consider the best way to organize support that will achieve the outlined objective.

Whole-staff inservice professional development and training is rarely, if ever, an effective method of providing technology training and support to teachers. This is the case for two reasons. Firstly, according to research (Whitehouse 2011), professional development that has the greatest impact on teaching practice is

- based on the needs of students and teachers;

- sustained;

- subject-specific;

- rooted in classroom practice;

- collaborative and reflective; and

- provided by external expertise.

One-off, whole-staff inservice often lacks, in particular, the sustained element that effective professional development requires. Teachers often feel that technology-specific whole-staff training is not sufficiently rooted in their specific subject or in classroom practice and that it fails to address *their* specific needs and the needs of their students.

At the practical level, when supporting teachers with technology in a whole-staff setting, there are simply too many people with varying needs trying to use devices with varying levels of comfort and needing vastly differing degrees of practical support. Needless to say, it can get messy and be seen by both those who are technology-competent and those who need to build their competence as being a waste of time. Wasting time is greatly annoying to teachers and will not help to promote a positive technology mindset!

When working to organize staff training or support, consider the following:

- What is the intention or objective of the training? Whose needs is it intended to meet?

- What forces are driving the need for this training: Internal or external? Top-down or bottom-up?

- What are the differentiated levels of training needed, and which teachers exist within those levels?

- What practice exists already within the staff or school that can support the training?

- How best can you differentiate the training to meet the needs of the staff?

- What follow-up will be necessary to support continual teacher development?

- Are you supporting teachers in the most effective way for them (coaching, modeling, providing professional development, etc.)?

Staff professional development is a continual process, and it should be needs-based, targeted, and purposeful, just as all teaching should be. As your staff's understanding and capacity with technology develops, so will the purposes and levels of differentiation needed within staff training.

Honor teacher agency.

As you work to create a culture of curiosity and professional dialogue related to technology within the school, be mindful to support teacher action and agency. There will, without a doubt, be teachers on your staff that are already using technology in the classroom or are eager to take a lead in supporting technology within the classroom. Be aware of those members of staff and support them in sharing practice, even becoming coaches or teacher-leaders. Often teachers are waiting for permission to try initiatives and take risks within the classroom. Remove barriers to allow for maximum excitement and participation.

Pedagogy

Pedagogy, naturally, is the backbone of schooling. How we teach and how our students learn are core aspects of what makes a school its unique self. How technology fits into that and how you as a leader support the pedagogical development of technology integration will have a significant impact on its efficacy. Chapters 3, 4, 5, and 6 describe in detail the rationale and approach we recommend for the pedagogy of technology integration. You can broadly support this pedagogical development in three ways:

- modeling

- teaching

- facilitating

Modeling

Aim to work with your staff the way you want your staff to work with the students. Even if, as a leader, you may at times feel removed from day-to-day learning, you have the advantage of having both the influence and the opportunity to teach and model for *staff* how technology can be used to enhance the learning process. These opportunities exist during whole-staff or team meetings, professional development days or sessions, or by highlighting and sharing examples of effective technology integration you see happening around the school. This can be within the classroom but also in the background of just about everything you do with your staff, from enhanced models of pedagogical practices to facilitating sharing of questions, feedback, or ideas. Be a model for how technology can be integrated, and be both transparent and explicit with your staff about how and why you are using these tools in your role as *their* teacher and leader.

By showcasing technology integration, you are not only supporting your staff's understanding but positioning yourself as a learner too. You are a leader, but your staff and even you should not expect that you know everything or are able to do everything well. It is OK to try new things with your staff and make mistakes. If you show agency and vulnerability, your staff will find courage in seeing you open yourself to implementing technology integration, and they will appreciate and respect your willingness to expose yourself to the risks and frustrations they may face in their technology-integration learning journey.

Teaching Staff to Identify Purpose, Barriers, and Opportunities

In Chapters 4 and 5, and in our supplement on enhancing teacher communication with technology (see the Online Resources), we went into further detail about the three Cs of student learning: communicating, collaborating, and constructing understanding.

We suggest that by using technology to enhance the processes of communicating and collaborating, teachers can better support their students in the ultimate goal of constructing understanding. In each chapter we gave illustrative examples of integration in action and guided teachers to identify the purposes, processes, opportunities, and barriers inherent in communication and collaboration for their students, as these are the places where technology might act as an enhancement to the learning process.

As a leader, you have direct knowledge of what the learning barriers and opportunities for students in your context are, from language or learning support needs to conceptual understandings. With this knowledge, you are in a position to tailor and deliver professional development based on these ideas to your teachers in a way that will be as meaningful and targeted as possible.

Teaching Staff to Plan and Scaffold Effectively

In Chapter 6 we suggested three main types of technology integration (single-lesson, embedded, and project-based) and provided a detailed six-step plan for integrating technology in the learning process, called the Intechgrate Approach (see Figure 9.5). The aim of this approach is to keep teachers focused on planning primarily for the core learning, or fundamental learning objective, while also scaffolding and planning for technology tools and skills that will support the core learning. You can support the pedagogical development of technology integration by finding and creating opportunities to explicitly teach your teachers how to integrate technology deliberately and effectively for the purposes best aligned with your school vision of technology in the classroom. Just like in any teaching scenario, a mixture of whole-group and differentiated-group teaching approaches will probably be most effective.

The Intechgrate Approach to Integrating Technology in the Classroom

Identify core learning → Outline the process → Plan and scaffold → Trouble-shoot and try out → Live the learning → Reflect

Continuously focus on core learning

Figure 9.5

Facilitating: Provide the Necessary Support

Different teachers will need different kinds of support from you as they work to apply their learning. Peer mentoring and coaching can help to support ongoing learning, and informal observations and regular check-ins about progress can provide teachers with an opportunity to raise practical concerns related to resources, infrastructure, or classroom management that might be hindering their attempts to integrate technology. Being actively involved in this way will also help you develop and maintain an understanding of what further training is needed for whom and what other elements of the Intechgrate Model may require attention (such as curriculum or infrastructure).

Above all, what teachers really need to know is that it is safe to take risks and that they are supported in trying new things and experiencing the inevitable failures that go along with trying new things. They need to know that you value the time they are investing and that what they are doing matters, both to you and to the school. This belief grows not only when teachers see firsthand that what they are doing with technology is making a difference to how students are learning but also from seeing that technology integration is an ongoing process in their school.

Curriculum

When discussing curriculum within Chapter 7, we focus on written curriculum, which we define as usually being composed of broad learning goals or standards that are further defined by clearer, more concise learning objectives. The outlined learning objectives may reference knowledge to be acquired as well as skills and understandings to be developed within a particular subject area.

Within most school contexts there are multiple pieces of the written curriculum, which we will reference in two categories: *general curriculum* (the so-called core academic curricula for English, math, social studies, etc.) and *technology-specific curriculum*.

As we have emphasized throughout this book, context is incredibly important, and this is particularly the case with regard to curriculum development and implementation. Many of the external system-level forces you identified at the beginning of this chapter are likely to have an impact on the curriculum you use and the degree of flexibility you as a leader have with which to approach it. In Chapter 7 we shared the elements we believe to be most critical when seeking to take a more integrated approach to the curricula you already have or design your own integrated technology curriculum.

Take a moment to consider the following questions:

- **What is the role of the curriculum within your school?**

- **Who has ownership of the curriculum?**

- **How and when is the curriculum referenced by staff?**

- **How do you support the use of curriculum materials within your interactions with staff?**

- **When is the curriculum revised?**

- **Do you have influence in the creation of the curriculum?**

Shifting Focus to an Integrated Approach to Curriculum

If you are working within a school where there are established general and technology-specific curricula, then you are in a perfect position to evaluate staff use of curricula and work to support a shift to a more integrated approach. This requires identifying learning within general curriculum subjects that can be enhanced when taught in parallel to aspects of the technology-specific curriculum—for example, using technology-specific learning outcomes for coding to enhance understanding of sequencing story events (English) or creating patterns (mathematics).

Once you have identified areas of commonality within the curricula, you can begin the process of finding a deliberate balance within the classroom teaching approach. Technology-specific and general curriculum learning will not always be balanced fifty-fifty, nor should they. Think of it more as a flexible scale or continuum: at times, the focus of the lesson might be 80 percent on the general curriculum, with technology acting as a support, and at other times that balance may be reversed. Being clear about the core learning (see Chapter 6, page 84) within the lesson will help to provide clarity regarding the use of technology.

Designing a Technology Curriculum for Integration

If you have flexibility within your technology curriculum, then you may be in the ideal position to build understanding and capabilities in staff as you lead its development or revision toward a more integrated technology curriculum.

As detailed in Chapter 7, a traditional technology curriculum is structured for the teaching of technology skills that the students will then be expected to apply at the needed time. An integrated technology curriculum is almost the exact opposite. We start by considering the broad intended learning for the students and then identify and articulate technology skills and understandings that would support that intended learning. In this way, the technology learning is framed by meaningful purpose for learning connected to a bigger concept.

By shifting from a skills-based technology curriculum to an integrated one that deliberately and explicitly places context and purpose at its center, it is easier for teachers to see and make connections to the general curriculum and therefore to plan for technology use and integration in a contextual and purposeful way. (For a more detailed description of an integrated technology curriculum, see Chapter 7.)

Moving Forward with Curriculum Writing

One of the keys to developing curriculum in a way that will lead to sustained implementation is to take sufficient time to plan the process of writing *and beyond*. Many leaders would agree that making changes is not the hardest part of school development. The real challenge is making changes that become sustainably embedded into how the school functions, the teachers teach, and the students learn. Implementation is not an event; it is a continual process, and successful curriculum development must reflect and respect that.

Throughout the planning, research, and writing process, invite relevant stakeholders to participate. Curriculum writing is not intended to be a solo venture: reach out and pull members of the school community into the process in a way that provides depth to the writing process and develops understanding in those involved. Remember those of your leadership and influencer team you identified earlier. Utilize and value the expertise and experiences that exist within your context, and this will both create buy-in at all levels and enrich the curriculum as a whole.

The design and implementation process

In Chapter 7, page 116, we shared our nine-step approach for designing and implementing an integration-focused technology curriculum. These steps are intended to guide schools and leaders through the process of researching, designing, implementing, and supporting technology curriculum development in a way that builds from core pedagogical beliefs and values the needs and strengths of different contexts and students. This will help you to both design and implement an integrated technology curriculum that is natural and sustainable.

Here's a brief overview of the nine steps:

1. Identify current technology beliefs and implementation.

2. Research a wide variety of approaches to technology integration locally and internationally.

3. Define or refine the vision for technology integration's purpose in your context.

4. Consider student need: how can technology help the needs of your specific students, and what do they need to know, learn, or be able to do?

5. Gather feedback and ideas from the wider school community on your plan thus far.

6. Create a curriculum writing plan and timeline, and assign areas of responsibility.

7. Draft, synthesize, gather teacher feedback, and redraft if necessary.

8. Implement, sustain, and embed.

9. Review, refine, and redraft the curriculum in an ongoing, planned way.

Designing, writing, and implementing curriculum will only be as strong as the support these processes receive. As a leader, helping staff to make curriculum a part of their everyday planning conversations will take conscious effort and time. Highlighting teachers' efforts and creating a platform for teachers to share their practice can boost confidence and make integrated technology teaching and learning visible. There is no end destination when it comes to technology, as it is always evolving, so pace both yourself and your staff so that integrating technology remains a journey.

Resources and Infrastructure

The technical and physical aspects of technology integration are just as important as the pedagogical ones. They have a profound impact on each other. For that reason, even if we feel that we lack the vocabulary, expertise, or ability to involve ourselves in the behind-the-scenes technical aspects of technology in education, it is important to try.

In Chapter 8 we referred to three technical aspects of technology: resources, infrastructure, and systems. *Resources* are the technology tools we tend to focus on, because of their visibility in schools, including physical, tangible things such as student and teacher devices, projectors and smartboards, speakers, and makerspaces. They also include, however, the less tangible things like technology staffing, time for training, and budget. *Infrastructure* refers to the generally less tangible but highly important technical elements such as Internet connection, Wi-Fi hot spots, the internal network, and the server, cabling, network, and switches hidden within the walls or in the basement that make everything work (or not work). *Systems* refers to the technology processes in place: how technical needs and errors are reported and responded to, how teachers access technology resources and request new ones, and aspects like budgetary planning for technology expenditure.

Leading a Pedagogical Approach to Technology

Most schools, of course, unless they are newly built or still in design stages, are unlikely to have been planned with today's technology or its integration in mind. As a result, something that many teachers and schools contend with is the reality that the technology that is in place does not match its desired educational purpose or does not function to the standard necessary to realize that purpose. Often, the response to this at a technical level is to suggest that teachers need to use the technology differently: adjust the vision, purpose, and use to work with the resources and infrastructure that are in place.

We call for a *pedagogical* approach to technology. This means beginning from the premise that if the purpose of a school is to support student learning, then the purpose of any resource in that school is also to support that goal. It is the job of technology to develop and adjust to meet student and teacher need, not the other way around.

To achieve this, it is critical to involve IT administrators and leaders in planning. These are key staff members who can help realize your and your team's desire for an integrated technology curriculum, and involving them early and often is paramount in moving a sustainable project forward.

You can develop, strengthen, and sustain the connections between the two worlds of IT and pedagogy by doing the following:

- Invite the IT leaders to observe or drop in on lessons with technology that demonstrate the purpose you have defined.

- Invite IT technicians and leaders to join teacher meetings or social events.

- Invite IT technicians and leaders to participate in school-based technology training sessions and workshops.

- Invite IT leaders to participate in curriculum review meetings or school development meetings.

- Seek opportunities to participate in IT discussions where possible.

- Plan regular catch-up or development meetings between pedagogical and technology leaders.

While actions like these will, over time, help to bridge the gap between the pedagogical purpose and the technical implementation, they also serve another important purpose. It is very helpful for both teachers and technical staff to understand the challenges each faces. It can be hard for technicians, for example, to appreciate the impact that a repeatedly dropping Internet connection can have on a lesson if they are not familiar with how students tend to respond to lesson disruptions or to appreciate the emotional and stressful impact on the teachers if they do not know the people whose planning time and teaching efforts have gone to waste. Likewise, it can be hard for teachers to understand why it is so frustrating for technical staff when resources are not used or returned correctly or why they can't resolve certain problems simply or quickly.

It is important that both groups build common appreciation that everyone is doing the very best they can and to see the humans behind the problems and solutions.

Encourage agency and empowerment

Regardless of your exact role in your school community, much of what is involved in leading a pedagogical approach to technology focuses not on technology but on the sense of empowerment and agency of your fellow staff members. Key to effecting change in relation to how technology functions at the practical, infrastructural level is having the belief that change is, in fact, possible. For teachers, a sense of helplessness or hopeless-ness can arise when they have lived with unreliable or unsuitable technology resources or infrastructure for any length of time. A pernicious belief can grow that *technology* is, in and of itself, unreliable or unsuitable. If there are problems with Internet speed, connectivity, device reliability, and so on, these generally exist at the local level. As such, the first step is to encourage your fellow teachers to feel empowered enough to raise the issue, seek to understand it, and find out what would be required to solve it. Most problems have solutions; the key is not accepting that the immediate, and probably isolated, *status quo* is unavoidable.

To help teachers to build that sense of agency and empowerment,

- make it clear how teachers can and should raise technology issues (e.g., the IT ticket system and whom to call);

- bring the IT specialists to a meeting so everyone knows the humans behind the technology; and

- encourage teachers to raise issues whenever they arise, even if this is repeatedly or frequently.

Of course, teachers are not the only ones who need that sense of agency and empowerment: leaders do too. In addition to the ideas for teachers, leaders can do the following:

- Take the time to get to know the infrastructure to whatever degree you can manage. How is it set up? What are the historic problems inherent in that setup? What are the long-term plans for infrastructural development?

- Make note of the terms that come up when discussing technology with specialists, and take time to learn some relevant vocabulary (e.g., What is a server? What are network switches?)

Most importantly, begin from the ideological position that the technology is there to meet the needs of your students and staff, not the other way around. That means insisting that resources and infrastructure that do not function as needed must have a plan for development, even if that plan may take a long time to realize.

Of course, there are exceptions to the "any problem can be solved" rule, such as in parts of the world in which technology is unreliable or unavailable because of lack of resources or support. In contexts like these, the question should be "How can we use what we have in the most effective way?" We can still build agency and empowerment in these situations by encouraging teachers to look for the best way to work within the situation.

Think strategically

One of the great challenges with technology purchasing and resourcing is the fact that technology changes so quickly. Infrastructure or resources purchased ten years ago are probably already obsolete, and even five years is a long time in the life of a device.

Furthermore, as your school's or context's understanding of—and vision for—technology's role in learning develops over time, with it the curriculum, needs, and capabilities of teachers and students will develop. To continue to meet demand and needs, the technology resources and infrastructure will need to develop and change as well, much to the chagrin of those who have only just reached a happy balance.

Nevertheless, it is important to try, as best as possible, to think about the long term and attempt to foresee the consequences of planned purchases and developments. For example, a lack of devices is most easily solved by buying more devices, but increasing devices has consequences for infrastructure and systems, in terms of Internet bandwidth, management of devices, apps and software licenses, and even the nuts and bolts of where those devices are stored and how they are accessed by teachers and students.

Planning for replacements and maintenance is also vital: devices today tend to have a reliable life span of three to five years. You must decide how to determine when devices have reached the end of that life span, what will happen to those devices when that time comes, and how you will afford and manage the ongoing funding of technology purchasing, replacing, and maintaining.

Focus on purpose

Sometimes the balance between purpose and tool can get away from all of us, teachers and leaders alike. Particularly in situations where top-down purchasing and provision is the standard approach to technology resourcing, it is easy to get into a situation where the technology is coming first, and the pedagogy is trying to adapt or keep up. It is most important that your focus as a leader remains on your stated purpose for technology integration and on guiding the development of physical technology to meet that purpose.

Technology development and resourcing should be purposeful, rather than reactionary (in response to an urgent but potentially temporary or non-learning-centered need or issue) or reflexive (thoughtless, not based in purpose, simply because funding is available or because something seems interesting or cool). Technology is a tool, not the star of the show.

Leadership

Effective technology integration leadership requires flexibility, sensitivity, and deliberateness in how you address the development needs of the different elements of the Intechgrate Model, from the organizational to the personal needs.

The nature of school development is that as you respond to one need, address one challenge, or capitalize on one strength, it will naturally change in response to your actions, with new needs, challenges, and strengths arising all the time. This phenomenon is not unique to technology, but perhaps the pace of change can be somewhat faster than in other areas of school, because technology itself changes so fast.

We sometimes liken this to a horse race with six horses, one for each element of the model (see Figure 9.6). Different elements, at different times, will pull into the lead, forcing the other horses to try to keep up. Just like in a real race, the horses will not, and cannot, all run at exactly the same rate at the same time toward a neck-and-neck joint victory, but they should, at least, all be running in the same direction! For example, as pedagogy develops and pulls ahead, this will put pressure on resources and curriculum to develop in response, such that they may even pull ahead of pedagogy and mindset. We hope, though, that the firm favorite to win will always be purpose, who leads the pack throughout.

Leading Technology Integration Is Like a Horse Race

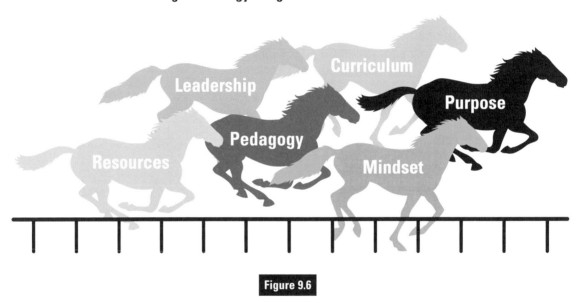

Figure 9.6

Leading and managing change in so many areas is no simple matter, but following are three key points to bear in mind as you consider how to do this going forward.

1. Meaningful Change Occurs in Response to Need

Lasting, meaningful change results from need and tension. Tension isn't necessarily comfortable, and it can be challenging on the personal level. However, it is through tension, and through challenges and by being uncomfortable sometimes, that we grow as people, as organizations, and as institutions. Don't feel that you need to keep ahead of tensions and needs: without them, there can't be growth. Instead, try to assess when technology wants become needs, and use these situations as opportunities to evaluate the status quo, reflect upon it, and make mindful, meaningful change that will support pedagogical purpose.

2. Leader-Led Isn't Necessarily Best

One of the most effective ways to kick-start a pedagogical shift in how technology is used and integrated is identifying an immediate need students and teachers have that could be quickly and simply solved by technology integration. For example, teachers take photos of learning, but they have no way of sharing those photos and rarely find the time to print them. This can be an opportunity to introduce a digital learning journal, with a small and open-minded group of teachers. Small pilot projects like this, which demonstrate clearly to teachers and students how the technology can make a difference in day-to-day learning and teaching, can create a surprisingly robust foothold for ongoing development, creating both interest and momentum.

3. You Should Control the Pace of Development

Strategic medium- to long-term action planning is vital to ensuring that changes are not overwhelming for teachers. In Chapter 7 we pointed out that implementing a new curriculum is not a matter of creating it and handing it out—it isn't an event, but rather a sustained process. Ongoing, lasting development is a sustained process too, of trial, error, reflection, refinement, continued attention and discussion, and embedment.

When we go too fast and change too much at one time, it can result in insufficient focus, at both the leadership and the teacher level, on aspects that really do need continued attention. It is better to invest time in shifting the mindset *before* investing in resources or addressing the curriculum, for example, and then ensure that when the curriculum and resources are developed, there is sufficient time and energy to invest in really exploring and embedding these aspects with a staff who is ready to use them.

You may have heard of change fatigue, a kind of apathy or passivity that affects members of an organization in which there have been repeated but unsustained efforts at change. Teachers are prone to this sort of fatigue because they have often been through many rounds of failed or stalled implementation of new educational ideas as new leadership or new governments have come and gone, and you may recognize this as an element of the technology mindset in your context.

However, it is important firstly to emphasize to teachers that developing a more effective approach to technology integration is *not* change—is it evolution and growth. The aim is not to add on a new initiative or tick a box, and it isn't going to go away when the principal changes or a new curriculum appears. It is about evolving our understanding and approach to technology's potential role in the big picture of student learning and working toward using it in as effective a way as possible, no matter what the specific technology is or what the specifics of the curriculum are.

Secondly, the leadership has a responsibility to prove that it really is development, and not arbitrary or temporary change, by

- clearly, deliberately, and repeatedly putting student learning front and center of plans for technology development; and

- committing to keeping technology integration a visible, sustained priority through discussions, pedagogical training, teacher goal setting, forward planning, and so on.

If we, as leaders, are going to ask teachers to commit to teaching differently with technology, we need to demonstrate a matching level of commitment to technology integration, because we are asking for a significant shift to take place in why and how they use technology for and with students. Like any pedagogical and ideological shift, it will take thought, work, and prioritization over an extended period of time, but it will be worthwhile.

As you move forward, we encourage you to do the following:

- Keep your valuable and intimate knowledge of your unique context front and center in your planning. What works for one school may not work for another, and you know your context best.

- Strive to maintain a balanced approach in terms of how you ask your staff to invest their time and energy. Not every element of development can happen as quickly or intensively as we might wish, but ultimately investing more time in a longer development process will likely result in more sustained and embedded change.

- Think strategically about every aspect. From pedagogical development, to training, to resources and infrastructure, to curriculum, each component of the Intechgrate Model affects and is affected by the others and requires careful thought.

- Remember the power you, as a leader, have to influence mindset, guide development, and encourage agency in those around you. Successful development in any area depends a great deal on the approach and attitudes of leaders. If you believe in the potential and importance of effective technology use and integration to support student learning, and you strive to realize that belief, you can make a positive difference in the experiences of the teachers and students in your school, whatever your leadership role may be.

Reflection

- *If your goal is student learning:* Do your personal beliefs align with the direction you see technology moving in schools? If not, how might this tension affect your leadership of technology in your context?

- How could you work collaboratively and collegially with members of your educational community to explore and define a vision for technology that will meet the needs of your students now and in the medium term?

- *If your goal is supporting professional learning:* How does technology mindset in your context support or hinder integration? How might you address negative elements of mindset in an inclusive, positive way?

- *If your goal is supporting curriculum development:* To what extent are your technology-specific curriculum (if you have one), your approach to technology within the general curricula, and your vision for technology integration aligned?

- *If your goal is supporting organizational systems and structures:* What are the major organizational barriers to effective technology integration that your context is facing right now (e.g., funding, staffing, sustainable budgeting, unreliable infrastructure)?

- Whom can you reach out to, to support you in addressing barriers beyond your own influence?

10

Taking
Integration
Forward

Reimagining technology's role in education means reviewing our shared understanding of what effective technology integration means, at the classroom level, at the school level, and at the educational-system level. Historically, the educational sector has looked at technology in education as a teaching issue, or a resourcing issue, or a curricular issue. We believe it is an all-encompassing educational issue, and addressing it means taking a holistic approach to considering how all the elements contribute to how meaningfully and effectively we teach—and our students learn—with and through technology.

In each of the preceding chapters of this book we have taken a deep dive into the six elements that make up what we call the Intechgrate Model. These six elements are each a crucial part of a jigsaw puzzle that come together to create the big picture of enhanced student learning. (See Figure 10.1.)

The Intechgrate Model: A Holistic Approach to Developing and Supporting Technology Integration in Education

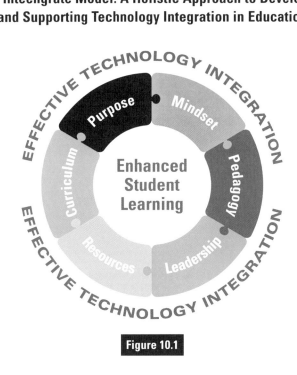

Figure 10.1

In a way, what we have done so far is to take that puzzle apart and look closely at the individual pieces, but now it is time to put it back together again and see how the whole picture looks from the perspective of your individual context. Where do you and your school stand in relation to the goal of enhancing student learning through technology integration?

Successful Technology Integration in Your Context

Having explored each element of the Intechgrate Model in depth, you may now be aware of some of the challenges and opportunities facing you as you begin or continue your journey of technology integration. To build on that awareness and help you turn it into a plan of action, we are going to do what is called a "force field analysis," first developed by Kurt Lewin (1951). A force field analysis is a way of analyzing the factors specific to you and your context that might have an impact on any development plan, in this case technology integration.

You can imagine these factors as being a bit like two teams playing tug-of-war (see Figure 10.2). In the middle of the rope, imagine that the arrow represents the status quo, the current situation. Imagine that on each side of the status quo are teams of factors pulling in opposite directions. On one side, the factors are pulling for development, to move the status quo toward change. On the other side, they are pulling to prevent development, to maintain the status quo and keep the situation as it is. Naturally, if there are more or stronger factors on one side or the other, this will affect the degree or rate of development that can occur.

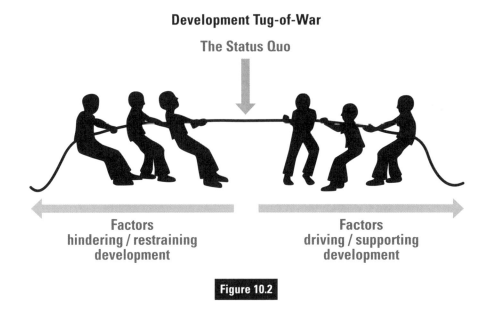

Development Tug-of-War

The Status Quo

**Factors
hindering / restraining
development**

**Factors
driving / supporting
development**

Figure 10.2

A tug-of-war is just one way of conceptualizing a force field analysis. You could also imagine the two opposing forces pushing toward each other, a set of scales with weights on either side, or something else entirely. Regardless of how you picture it, the important thing about the analysis is that it encourages you to identify the factors that might be hindering progress *and* the ones that could support it. It is certainly important to be aware of problems and challenges so we can look for solutions, but if we forget to leverage and build on the advantages we have available to us, then we are seeing only half the picture and are missing out on valuable opportunities.

Throughout this book you may have noticed a theme: we recognize that schools are highly contextual places and the challenges and opportunities in each of those contexts are utterly unique. The wonderful thing about a force field analysis is that it is also unique: it encourages you to consider what forces are hindering and supporting development in your own specific context.

By now you will hopefully have a clear idea of where you or your school or context currently is regarding technology integration. This is the status quo. In Figure 10.3, take a few minutes to note down for yourself what the status quo currently is, considering each element of the Intechgrate Model (printable version of Figure 10.3 available in the Online Resources).

Considering the Status Quo in Your Context

Considering the Status Quo in Your Context

THE STATUS QUO
(WHAT IS YOUR CURRENT SITUATION?)

Purpose

Mindset

Pedagogy

Curriculum

Resources and Infrastructure

Leadership

© 2020 by Sarah Gilmore and Katierose Deos from Integrating Technology. Portsmouth, NH: Heinemann.

Integrating Technology Online Resources

To access a downloadable and printable version of Figure 10.3 from the online resources, either scan the QR code on page ix or visit Hein.pub/Tech-Resources

Figure 10.3

Next you are going to identify the factors you recognize as hindering and driving the development of technology integration in your context. Figures 10.4 and 10.5 provide two different approaches for you to choose from (printable versions also available in the Online Resources), depending on how you conceptualize this, or you might prefer to create your own on blank paper.

Force Field Analysis Template 1

<table>
<tr><th colspan="2" align="center">Force Field Analysis Template 1</th></tr>
<tr><th align="center">FACTORS HINDERING OR
RESTRAINING DEVELOPMENT</th><th align="center">FACTORS DRIVING OR
SUPPORTING DEVELOPMENT</th></tr>
</table>

© 2020 by Sarah Gilmore and Katierose Deos from Integrating Technology. Portsmouth, NH: Heinemann.

Integrating Technology
Online Resources

To access a downloadable and printable version of Figures 10.4 and 10.5 from the online resources, either scan the QR code on page ix or visit Hein.pub/Tech-Resources

Figure 10.4

You are unlikely to have an equal number of factors on each side, and of course, not every factor on each side is equally strong. Just like in tug-of-war, one very strong factor on one side might well outpull several less powerful factors on the other side. You could try representing what you consider to be the relative strength of different powers by noting them in different sizes, by assigning a subjective numerical value to each, or by using a different method that makes the most sense to you.

While you are thinking about this, here are a few points to bear in mind:

- Consider all the elements of the Intechgrate Model (purpose, mindset, pedagogy, curriculum, resources and infrastructure, and leadership) as you do this.

Force Field Analysis Template 2

The Status Quo

| Factors
hindering / restraining
development | Factors
driving / supporting
development |

Figure 10.5

- Remember to look just as hard for those factors that will drive and support development as those that might hold it back.

- You may find that an identified factor supports and hinders development in different ways at the same time. For example, if your school is required to implement educational legislation, this can hinder development as it requires staff time and energy, but it can also support development because through the new educational legislation you, as a school, have increased ownership over curriculum development. Or, imagine that your school district has decided to have a district-wide focus on narrative writing for the academic year. This can hinder development as staff meetings and staff training will be focused on narrative writing, but this can also support development by providing your staff with a technology integration focus (narrative writing) for the academic year.

- In schools in particular, people are often our greatest resource. Who are the people who are likely to be your champions for change?

- Schools are made up of more than teachers and leaders—they are communities! Think about parents, students, administrators, and the wider educational network.

How Should You Address the Factors Influencing Integration?

With what is hopefully now a clearer picture of what factors are standing between you and moving the status quo toward successful technology integration, as well as what factors could support that goal, you can now begin to make a plan to move forward.

The table in Figure 10.6 is an example of a format you could use to organize the hindering and driving factors you have identified and begin to consider how you might address or build upon them. When you are thinking about the factors and the action that you could take to address or build on them, you might want to revisit relevant chapters of the book. In each chapter we have offered suggestions for addressing aspects related to each of the elements of the Intechgrate Model. Naturally, not all of those suggestions will work in every educational situation or context, but we hope they have given you ideas you can adapt to suit your unique needs.

For example, if low technology competency or reluctance to use technology is a hindering issue, you could revisit Chapter 3, where we explore technology mindset. That might guide you to consider what options there might be for upskilling through mentoring, peer coaching, or differentiated training workshops.

Whether you have identified three action points or thirty, and whether you are thinking at the individual classroom level or an organizational level or even beyond, it is important to bear in mind that it is not going to be possible to address all of these points at once. Even if it were possible, it wouldn't be wise as you can devote only so much time, energy, and focus to development of this type without risking fatigue or disillusionment. Additionally, development is best undertaken at a considered, strategic pace: sudden or extreme changes in pedagogy, approach, or curriculum have a tendency to fizzle out and never move beyond the implementation stage to becoming truly sustainable and embedded.

Try to pick a place to start that seems manageable. We have found that one way of doing this is to identify an action point that might relate to a current, burning need or a question in the classroom. By finding a sensible and sustainable technology-based solution to even a seemingly minor daily classroom problem, you can plant a seed that shows the potential of technology for learning and teaching and sets the proverbial ball rolling.

Force Field Analysis Planning Table

FACTOR AND RELATED INTECHGRATE MODEL ELEMENT	SUPPORTING OR HINDERING?	ACTION YOU COULD TAKE
Force Field Analysis Planning Table		

Integrating Technology Online Resources

To access a downloadable and printable version of Figure 10.6 from the online resources, either scan the QR code on page ix or visit Hein.pub/Tech-Resources

Figure 10.6

What's Next? Intechgrate in Your School

We believe that technology can make a real difference in the lives and learning of teachers and students around the world. We also believe that no matter where you and your school are right now in your journey with technology integration, no matter what you have and what you need, there are positive steps you can take to make technology integration a more meaningful force for student learning.

In order for that goal to become a reality educators need to take a holistic view of technology in education. We hope that this book has communicated a clear vision for that, as well as provided you with ideas, tools, and questions to take your personal understanding of technology integration forward.

Thinking about technology integration in this new way, and considering what you as a teacher or a leader need or want to do to achieve this goal, might well be daunting! With so many interconnected yet equally individually important elements to consider, you might worry at times that effective technology integration is an unattainable goal, but we want to reassure you that it *is* attainable, and it *is* worth the effort.

As you begin or continue your journey with technology integration, remember that you aren't on your own: there is a whole community of like-minded educators out there who are on the same journey you are. Even if those educators are not right next to you in your grade level, school, or physical context, you can create a supportive network of colleagues online and through social media.

Connect with educators, ask questions, share stories, and more on Twitter using the hashtag #Intechgrate or join the Facebook group at https://www.facebook.com /groups/IntechgrateBookCommunity.

The task of reimagining the role of technology in education is a journey that we encourage the entire educational community to undertake together. Like many journeys, this one is likely to have delays and detours, as well as successes and awakenings, and it can happen only one step at a time. Meaningful, lasting change is never quick or easy, but each step we take brings us closer to a future where technology fulfills its potential as a truly purposeful, meaningful tool to enhance student learning.

Works Cited

AAP Council on Communications and Media. 2016. "Media and Young Minds." *Pediatrics* 138 (5): e20162591. doi:10.1542/peds.2016-2591. https://pediatrics.aappublications.org/content/138/5/e20162591.

Albion, Peter R., Jo Tondeur, Alona Forkosh-Baruch, and Jef Peeraer. 2015. "Teachers' Professional Development for ICT Integration: Towards a Reciprocal Relationship Between Research and Practice." *Education and Information Technologies* 20 (4): 655–73.

Carlsson-Paige, Nancy, Geralyn Bywater McLaughlin, and Joan Wolfsheimer Almon. 2015. *Reading Instruction in Kindergarten: Little to Gain and Much to Lose*. Annapolis, MD, and Jamaica Plain, MA: Alliance for Childhood and Defending the Early Years.

Claxton, Guy. 2017. *The Learning Power Approach: Teaching Learners to Teach Themselves*. Thousand Oaks, CA: Corwin.

Costa, Arthur L., and Bena Kallick, eds. 2008. *Learning and Leading with Habits of Mind: 16 Essential Characteristics for Success*. Alexandria, VA: ASCD.

Dickens, Charles. 2017 (originally published 1859). *Hunted Down*. Brooklyn, NY: Sheba Blake.

Drent, Marjolein, and Martina Meelissen. 2008. "Which Factors Obstruct or Stimulate Teacher Educators to Use ICT Innovatively?" *Computers and Education* 51 (1): 187–99.

Ertmer, Peggy A. 2005. "Teacher Pedagogical Beliefs: The Final Frontier in Our Quest for Technology Integration?" *Education Technology Research and Development* 53 (4): 25–39.

Gardner, Howard. 2011. *Frames of Mind: The Theory of Multiple Intelligences*. New York: Basic Books.

Helsper, Ellen J., and Rebecca Eynon. 2010. "Digital Natives: Where Is the Evidence?" *British Educational Research Journal* 36 (3): 503–20.

Hermans R., J. Tondeur, J. van Braak, and M. Valcke. 2008. "The Impact of Primary School Teachers' Educational Beliefs on the Classroom Use of Computers." *Computers and Education* 51 (4): 1499–509.

International Society for Technology in Education (ISTE). 2016. "ISTE Standards for Students." www.iste.org/standards/for-students.

Kaye, Cathryn Berger. 2010. *The Complete Guide to Service Learning*. Golden Valley, MN: Free Spirit.

Keene, Ellin Oliver, and Susan Zimmermann. 1997. *Mosaic of Thought: Teaching Comprehension in a Reader's Workshop*. Portsmouth, NH: Heinemann.

Larose, Simon, Donald U. Robertson, Roland Roy, and Frederic Legault. 1998. "Nonintellectual Learning Factors as Determinants for Success in College." *Research in Higher Education* 39 (3): 275–97.

Lewin, Kurt. 1951. *Field Theory in Social Science*. New York: Harper & Row

Manning, Ellen. 2017. "Out with the Old School? The Rise of Ed Tech in the Classroom." *The Guardian*, August 1. www.theguardian.com/small-business-network/2017/aug/01/schools-slowly-edtech-sector-cubetto-kahoot-firefly.

McDermott, Nick. 2018. "Switch Off: Kids Who Spend Too Much Time Staring at Screens 'at Greater Risk of 12 Deadly Cancers.'" *The Sun*, November 7. www.thesun.co.uk/news/7676521/kids-staring-screens-too-long-risk-cancer/.

Orben, Amy, and Andrew K. Przybylski. 2019. "The Association Between Adolescent Well-Being and Digital Technology Use." *Nature Human Behaviour* 3: 173–82.

Organisation for Economic Co-operation and Development (OECD). 2019. "Distribution of Teachers by Age and Gender." OECD.Stat Web Browser. https://stats.oecd.org/Index.aspx?DataSetCode=EAG_PERS_SHARE_AGE.

———. 2015. *Students, Computers and Learning: Making the Connection*. Paris: OECD.

Papert, Seymour. 1980. *Mindstorms: Children, Computers, and Powerful Ideas*. New York: Basic Books.

Pedder, David, Anne Storey, and V. Darleen Opfer. 2008. *Schools and Continuing Professional Development (CPD) in England—State of the Nation Research Project*. Cambridge and Milton Keynes, England: University of Cambridge and the Open University.

Perkins, David. 2003. "Making Thinking Visible." www.pz.harvard.edu/resources/making-thinking-visible-article-0.

Perkins, David, Shari Tishman, and Ron Ritchhart. 2000. "Intelligence in the Wild: a Dispositional View of Intellectual Traits." *Educational Psychology Review* 12 (3): 269–93.

Prestridge, Sarah. 2010. "The Alignment of Digital Pedagogy to Current Teacher Beliefs." Paper presented at Australian Computers in Education Conference 2010, Melbourne, April 6–9. Available at https://pdfs.semanticscholar.org/7327/38ef777521fc8c4cca509d254027825f116b.pdf?_ga=2.148066039.1983543885.1556610713-375085899.1556610713.

———. 2012. "The Beliefs Behind the Teacher That Influences Their ICT Practices." *Computers and Education* (58) 1: 449–58.

Ritchhart, Ron. 2015. *Creating Cultures of Thinking: The 8 Forces We Must Master to Truly Transform Our Schools*. San Francisco: Jossey-Bass.

Ritchhart, Ron, Mark Church, and Karin Morrison. 2011. *Making Thinking Visible: How to Promote Engagement, Understanding, and Independence for All Learners*. San Francisco: Jossey-Bass.

Sang, Guoyuan, Martin Valcke, Johan van Braak, Jo Tondeur, and Zhu Chang. 2010. "Predicting ICT Integration into Classroom Teaching in Chinese Primary Schools: Exploring the Complex Interplay of Teacher-Related Variables." *Journal of Computer Assisted Learning* 27 (2): 160–72.

Stember, Marilyn. 1991. "Advancing the Social Sciences Through the Interdisciplinary Enterprise." *The Social Science Journal* 28 (1): 1–14.

Tough, Paul. 2014. *How Children Succeed: Grit, Curiosity and the Hidden Power of Character*. New York: Mariner Books

Whitehouse, Claire. 2011. "Effective Continuing Professional Development for Teachers: Executive Summary." Manchester, England: Centre for Research and Practice (CERP) AQA. https://cerp.aqa.org.uk/sites/default/files/pdf_upload/CERP-RP-CW-19052011.pdf.

Wiggins, Grant, and Jay McTighe. 2011. *The Understanding by Design Guide to Creating High-Quality Units*. Alexandria, VA: ASCD.

World Cancer Research Fund. 2018. "Diet, Nutrition and Physical Activity: Energy Balance and Body Fatness. The Determinants of Weight Gain, Overweight and Obesity." www.wcrf.org/sites/default/files/Energy-Balance-and-Body-Fatness.pdf